Anonymous

The Practical Home Cook-Book

With useful instructions on marketing and the choice of articles of food

Anonymous

The Practical Home Cook-Book
With useful instructions on marketing and the choice of articles of food

ISBN/EAN: 9783744789141

Printed in Europe, USA, Canada, Australia, Japan

Cover: Foto ©Lupo / pixelio.de

More available books at **www.hansebooks.com**

THE

PRACTICAL HOME

l f

COOK-BOOK.

WITH USEFUL INSTRUCTIONS ON MARKETING AND THE CHOICE
OF ARTICLES OF FOOD.

IT CONTAINS THE FOLLOWING:

*HOW TO MAKE SOUPS, BROTHS, STEWS, HASHES,
AND SAVORY DISHES; HOW TO DRESS VEGETA-
BLES, ROASTING, BOILING, FRYING, BROIL-
ING AND SAUCES, POULTRY AND GAME;
FISH, PIES, PUDDINGS; PASTRY; CON-
FECTIONERY; BREAD; ETC.;
HOW TO PICKLE; HOW
TO PRESERVE AND
BOTTLE FRUIT;
ETC., ETC.*

EXAMINE THE CONTENTS.

NEW YORK:
NEW YORK POPULAR PUBLISHING CO.
MAIN OFFICE, 37 Bond St.
COLORING, PRINTING AND ENGRAVING DEP'TS, 18 Rose St.

A. J DICK,
E. J. STECHER, } . . . . Proprietors.

CONTENTS.

(Each Recipe is Numbered.)

―――――◆●▶―――――

CONTENTS.—CONTINUED.

PICKLING AND PRESERVING.

CONTENTS.

CONTENTS—CONTINUED

DOMESTIC COOKERY.

ON THE CHOICE OF ARTICLES OF DIET.

To Choose Beef.—Good ox beef has an open grain, and yields easily to the pressure of the finger; it is smooth and juicy, of a rich carnation-color in the lean, and the fat is of a fine cream-color; rich without being oily, firm without being hard. It is small in the bone, and full in the flesh.

Mutton.—In choosing mutton select that which is of a rich red color, close in the grain and of a silky texture, juicy and lively in appearance, and whitish in the fat, but not shiny and tallowy. The flesh should pinch tender, and rise again when dented.

Lamb.—Observe the neck vein in the fore-quarter, which should be of an azure-blue to denote quality and sweetness. The flesh should be light-colored and juicy, the fat white and rich, the bones thin and small. Lamb should be dressed while perfectly fresh, or the flavor will be destroyed. It is in season from April till August.

Venison.—Pass a knife along the bones of the haunches and shoulders; if it smells sweet, the meat is new and good; if tainted, the fleshy parts of the sides will look discolored, and the darker in proportion to its staleness. The clefts of the hoofs of young venison are close and smooth. The buck venison is in full season from May till Allhallows; the doe, from Michaelmas to December or January.

Veal.—The lean of good, well-fed veal is white, smooth, and juicy; the fat is white, firm, and abundant. The flesh of a bull-calf is firmer and of a deeper color than that of a cow-calf, and the fat is harder; they are equally good for eating, if young and well-fed. It is easy to tell whether veal be newly killed, or stale, by its general appearance, as the color changes quickly, particularly under the kidney and the flaps of the breast. The flesh of stale-killed veal feels moist and clammy, the joints flabby and pliable, and it has a faint, musty smell.

Pork.—If young and well-fed, the lean is easily broken between the fingers, and the skin indented if nipped with the nail; the fat is white and waxy, and the rind thin and clean. Stale-killed pork is easily detected by the skin looking dark on the top, and clammy between the creases of the legs and shoulders, and by its strong, tainted smell. Pork is in season from August till March.

Ham and Bacon.—Run a knife along the bone of a ham; if it come out clean, and have a savory flavor, the ham is good; if smeared and dulled, it is spoiled either by taint or is reasty. Hocks and gammons of bacon may be proved in the same way.

Good bacon is red in the lean, and the fat is white, firm, and pulpy; the rind is fine and thin. If it be sheathed with yellow, it is reasty and unfit for use.

Poultry.—In selecting poultry choose those that are full-grown, but not old. When young and fresh-killed the eyes are full and bright, the joints neither stiff nor flabby; the skin thin and tender, so that it may be easily torn with a pin; the breast-bone is pliable, yielding easily to pressure. Fowls, if young, have a hard, close vent, and the legs and comb are smooth. A goose, if young, has but few hairs, a yellow bill, and is limber-footed. Ducks, when fat, are hard and thick on the belly; if young and good they are limber-footed.

Eggs.—Put your tongue to the larger end: if it feel warm, the egg is fresh; or put the egg into a pan of cold water; if perfectly fresh it will sink immediately, and so in proportion to its freshness; a rotten egg will float en the top of the water.

Butter.—The only way to try butter is by the smell and taste; never trust to its external appearance. Do not buy that which is speckled with pinky spots, nor that which has a milky appearance; such butter has not been well washed from the butter-milk, and will quickly turn sour or lose its flavor.

Fish.—The best are thick and firm. When fresh they have stiff fins, bright scales, red gills, and eyes full and bright. Freshness is best indicated by the smell. In proportion to the time they have been out of the water they are soft and flabby, the fins pliable, the scales dim, the gills dark, and the eyes sunken. Cod, turbot, &c., should be firm, white, clear, and transparent. Salmon, mackerel, herrings, &c., are chosen by their brightness and brilliancy of color. Shell-fish, such as lobsters and crabs, can only be chosen by the smell, and by opening them at the joint to discover whether or not they are well-filled, for they sometimes feel heavy through being charged with water. If a lobster be fresh, the tail will be stiff, and spring back sharply if pulled up. A *cock* lobster may be known by the narrowness of the back part of his tail and the stiffness of the two uppermost fins within it, while those of a *hen* are soft, and the back of her tail is broader.

SOUPS AND BROTHS.

GENERAL REMARKS.—The chief art in making good soup lies in the judicious blending of the different flavors, so that nothing shall predominate.

The scum should be taken off before the soup boils, or it will not be clear. All the fat is to be taken off. Simmer very softly. If soup be suffered to boil quickly, the goodness of the meat can never be extracted.

Put the meat into cold water; let it be long on the fire before it comes to a boil; allow about two tablespoonfuls of salt to a gallon of soup, if it have many vegetables; less if the vegetables be few. From a pint and a half to a quart of water to every pound of meat will make good soup. If the water waste, and more is to be added, use boiling water. Cold or lukewarm water will spoil the soup. Keep the saucepan in which your soup is boiling closely covered, or the strength will fly off with the steam.

Soup will be as good the second day as the first, if heated to the boiling-point. It should never be left in the saucepan but should be turned into a dish or shallow pan, and set aside to get cold. Never cover it up, as that will cause it to turn sour very quickly.

Before heating a second time, remove all the fat from the top. If this be melted in, the flavor of the soup will certainly be spoiled.

Thickened soups require nearly double the seasoning used for thin soup or broth.

Brown soup is made chiefly of beef; white soup of veal.

1. *To Make Stock.*—Bone a leg or shin of beef of ten pounds' weight, saw the bone in three, and take out the marrow. Put the bone into a saucepan with six quarts of water, and set it on to boil. Put the marrow into another saucepan with the meat, cut up small, and a pound of lean ham or bacon; turn it well about till it is fried a nice brown, then add the liquor from the bones, cover up the pot and simmer for four or five hours. Strain it through a hair-sieve, and set it by till cold; the fat may then be taken off, and it will be ready for any soup that may be required. This forms the foundation of gravy, ox-tail, vegetable, and other soups.

2. *Mock Turtle Soup.*—Take a calf's head, the skin having been scalded and the hair scraped off clean, wash it thoroughly; take out the brains and boil them separately till done enough. Put the head into a pot with more water than will cover it. Skim it frequently till it boils, and let it boil for an hour, but very gently. Take it out, and when cool, cut the meat into pieces of about an inch square. Scrape and cut the tongue in the same manner. Lay all these pieces aside, then put into the water in which the head was boiled, about three or four pounds of leg of beef and a knuckle of veal—the meat cut small and the bones broken. Add four or five onions, a carrot and turnip, sliced, a small bunch of sweet herbs, and some whole black and Jamaica pepper. Boil all together slowly, for four or five hours, then strain it and let it cool, when take off the fat. Now melt a lump of butter in a stew-pan, put to it two handfuls of flour, and let it brown, stirring it all the time. Add a little of the soup, a sprig or two of sweet basil, and a few sprigs of parsley. Boil this for a quarter of an hour, strain it through a sieve, put it with the pieces of meat, into the soup, with the brains pounded, and boil all together for an hour. Add half a teacupful of catsup, the juice of a lemon, cayenne pepper, and salt, to taste, also four glasses of sherry, and when dished in a tureen, put in two dozen of force-meat balls, and the same quantity of egg-balls, which are made as follows:

3. *Egg Balls.*—Boil four or five eggs till they are quite hard. Take out the yolks and beat them in a mortar, with salt and cayenne pepper. Make this into a paste with the white of egg. Roll the paste into balls the size of small marbles. Roll them in a little flour and fry them in butter, taking care they do not break.

4. *Force-meat Balls.*—Cut half a pound of veal and half a pound of suet fine, and beat them in a mortar. Have a few sweet herbs shred fine; dried mace beaten fine; a small nutmeg grated; a little

lemon-peel cut very fine; a little pepper and salt, and the yolks of two eggs; mix all these well together, then roll them in little round balls; roll them in flour and fry them brown. If for white sauce, put them in a little boiling water, and boil them for a few minutes, but do not fry them.

5. *Ox-tail Soup.*—Make a quantity of brown soup with shin of beef; take two or three tails and cut them in pieces at the joints; put them into the soup and stew them till tender, but not till the meat leaves the bones. Add a little catsup, and serve it with the pieces of tail in the soup.

6. *Vegetable Soup.*—Take the liquor in which any meat has been boiled; cut into it two onions, two turnips, a large carrot, a head of celery, and a little parsley; add also a bunch of sweet herbs; boil all together for a couple of hours; then take out the sweet herbs and rub the vegetables through a sieve; have ready some chopped parsley, and boil all up again. Season with pepper and salt. Thicken, if required, with barley, rice, or sago. This soup may be made better by cutting into it a pound or two of lean beef.

7. *Mutton Broth.*—This is an excellent broth for invalids, being of a very mild nature, and particularly efficacious to those whose stomachs have been rendered tender by much medicine. The best parts of mutton for making broth are either the scrag end of the neck or the chump end of the loin, which should be put into a clean saucepan with cold water in the proportion of a quart of water to every pound of meat. Throw in a little salt and skim it well as it comes to a boil; then set it aside that it may simmer very gently; slice in an onion and two turnips; let it stew for two hours, and, just before you take it up, chop up a few sprigs of parsley very fine, and put into the broth, first taking out the mutton. Toast some bread in thin slices, and cut it in small squares into a basin; pour the broth over it, and serve the meat in a dish. The turnips may be strained dry and served plain, or mashed up with a little butter, pepper, and salt. Some prefer to thicken the broth with pearl barley. If for a sick person, omit the herbs and vegetables.

8. *Beef Tea.*—Take a pound of lean beef, cut it small, and put it with a quart of cold water, into a saucepan; add a little salt and two or three allspice. Put it on a slow fire and skim it carefully as it comes to a boil. Let it simmer gently for an hour, then strain it through a hair sieve. Some persons cut in a small onion, but that is scarcely fit for invalids.

9. *Beef Broth.*—Take a leg of beef, cut it in pieces; put it into a gallon of water; skim it; put in two or three blades of mace, some parsley, and a crust of bread; boil it till the beef and sinews are tender. Toast bread and cut into dice; put it in a dish; lay in the beef, and pour on the broth.

10. *Pea Soup.*—This soup should be made with liquor in which any kind of meat has been boiled, but the liquor of salt pork gives it a more savory flavor. It can be made with water alone, if you have no pot-liquor; but in that case it is better to get a few bones, as they will add greatly to the flavor and nourishing qualities of the soup. Wash one quart of peas perfectly clean, put them into

a pot with the bones and three carrots sliced thin, and simmer gently for about an hour; then add four onions cut in thin slices, a head of celery, a few sweet herbs, and a few sprigs of parsley chopped very fine, and let the whole stew gently for three hours longer, taking care to stir it now and then, as the peas are apt to burn. Press the whole through a colander with a spoon, season it with pepper and salt to your palate, put it over the fire again to have it quite hot, and serve it up with some thin toasted bread and some dried mint rubbed fine.

It should be observed, that split peas will not soften in salt liquor; therefore, if you make your soup of salt pork or salt beef liquor, it will be necessary to boil the peas by themselves in a small quantity of soft water until they are melted; the vegetables meantime will be cooking in the liquor, and the peas, when sufficiently done, must be added. Green peas make an excellent soup in summer. The peas are boiled to a pulp and then rubbed through a sieve, afterwards flavored with pepper and salt.

STEWS, HASHES, AND SAVORY DISHES.

GENERAL REMARKS.—Hashing meat is a method of re-cooking dressed meat. The meat ought never to be suffered to boil, or it will become hard and tasteless. The gravy should be made first; the flour and all the ingredients added to flavor it, should be properly cooked; the meat should then be put in, and just heated through.

Stews are made of uncooked meat, and require very little water, delicate and savory seasoning, and thorough, though slow cooking, so as to render the meat soft and tender. The butter which is added to make a stew rich should be melted, not oiled, nor in too great quantity; all the fat of the meat should be skimmed clean off, and the flour for thickening should be added gradually, in order to avoid lumps, which, when once formed, can only be dissolved by rubbing through a hair sieve.

The seasoning depends on the judgment and taste of the cook. All the flavors should be made to blend in harmony; neither the pepper, salt, spice, herbs, nor any of the vegetables, should be suffered to predominate.

Stews may be thickened with flour, rice, arrowroot, or barley.

11. *For Browning and Thickening Gravy or Soup.*—Take a lump of butter the size of an egg, put it into a stewpan with a tablespoonful of sugar, and stir them together till they become of a dark brown, then dredge in sufficient flour to thicken it.

12. *To Make Brown Gravy.*—Cut the meat into pieces, season it with pepper and salt, and put it into a saucepan with a lump of butter; fry it quite brown, taking care that it does not stick to the pot; pour boiling water to it, a pint to each pound; let it simmer three hours, skimming it clean, then let it stand and settle; strain and set it aside for use. Thicken it as required.

13. *To Make Gravy for a Hash of Cold Meat.*—Cut a small onion into quarters or slices and fry it in a saucepan with a lump of butter; add a sufficient quantity of water, pepper, and salt,

and a spoonful of catsup; let it boil till the onion is tender, strain the gravy and thicken it with flour; let it boil a little longer, then add the meat, which is to be heated quite through, but not to be suffered to boil.

14. *Curries and Curry Powder.*—Chickens, rabbits, and veal are most suitable for curry. Boil the meat till tender, then separate the joints, put the meat into a stew-pan with a lump of butter and a little of the liquor in which it was boiled, and stew it for twenty minutes longer; then to four pounds of meat take a tablespoonful of curry powder, a teacupful of boiled rice, a tablespoonful of flour and one of melted butter, a teacupful of the liquor and half a teaspoonful of salt; mix them, and stew the meat in the liquor for ten minutes, when it will be ready to serve. Boiled rice is served as an accompaniment.

15. *Curry Powder.*—Coriander seed and tumeric, of each three ounces; ginger, pepper, and mustard, of each one ounce; half an ounce of cardamons; cayenne pepper, cinnamon, and cumin-seed, of each a quarter of an ounce. Pound them fine, sift, and bottle the mixture, then cork tight.

16. *To Hash Cold Meat.*—Cut the meat in thin slices off the bones, and lay it on a dish; sprinkle on some pepper and salt; put the bones into a pot with a little water; slice in a small onion, and let them stew to make gravy; take out the bones, and thicken the gravy with a little flour; add also a spoonful of catsup, boil it up, and then lay in your meat; shake it all up, and let it get hot through. Pour it into a dish on some thin snippets of bread.

17. *Minced Veal.*—Cut the meat from the bones, and, having minced it very fine with a small piece of lemon-peel and a sprig or two of parsley, grate over it a little nutmeg, and sprinkle on some pepper and salt; now put the bones into the saucepan with a small onion split in four, a sprig of savory, and one of marjoram; stew them to make gravy. When done, strain it off, and thicken it with a little flour and butter, give it a boil up, then turn in your mince, shake all well together, and let it get thoroughly hot, but do not to suffer it to boil; pour it over some thin toasted bread. Fry thin rashers of bacon, and lay them round the dish.

18. *Alamode Beef.*—Take a piece of clod or sticking of beef and cut it in small pieces, then put a lump of dripping into your pot with a good-sized onion cut thin; when quite hot roll the pieces of beef in flour and lay them in, stirring it well about; when nicely browned all over, add boiling water, in the proportion of a quart to every pound of meat: this must be added by degrees, and the whole kept stirring well together all the time; then put in a few allspice, two bay-leaves, some black pepper, and a little salt; cover it up close, and set it by the side of the fire, so that it may stew very gently till the meat becomes quite tender, which it will in about three hours, when it will be ready to serve up.

19. *Stewed Brisket of Beef.*—Put a piece of brisket of beef, say of four pounds' weight, into a saucepan with a good lump of dripping or butter; brown it well all over, then pour in as much water as will nearly cover the meat, and, closing the lid tight, stew it gently for three hours, taking care that the meat does not burn to the pot, which may be prevented by putting a small

plate beneath it. Boil a carrot, two turnips, and a few very small onions in another saucepan, just before you intend to serve up the dinner; take a cupful of the liquor and mix in it two good tablespoonfuls of flour, some pepper and salt, and a little catsup; turn this, with the onions and the carrot, and the turnips cut in small squares, into the pot with the meat, and, shaking it well up, boil all together for a few minutes, when it will be ready. Should the beef be fat, the gravy will require skimming, which must be done before you add the thickening.

20. *Savory Stewed Steak.*—Take some slices of beef, pepper and salt them well, slice up a couple of onions thin, and lay a piece or two of the fat of the steak at the bottom of a clean saucepan, then some of the onion, and on that some more steak, and so on alternately till you have put all in; shake and turn it about frequently to keep it from burning; it will presently be nice and brown; let it stew in its own gravy till the meat becomes tender, then take off all the fat from the top, mix some flour in two table-spoonfuls of water, with a little catsup or pickled walnut liquor, and pour it gradually into the stew; stir it about well, and just give it a boil up, serve it quite hot.

21. *Stewed Knuckle of Veal.*—Let the saucepan be perfectly clean; wash the knuckle well; place four wooden skewers at the bottom of the pot, to prevent the meat burning; lay in your veal with two or three blades of mace, an onion, a little whole pepper, a sprig of thyme and some salt, with two quarts of water; cover it close, and let it simmer gently for two hours; when done enough, lay in it a dish, and strain the broth over it. The shoulder is very good stuffed and stewed.

22. *Ragout of Rabbit.*—Wash and clean a good rabbit; boil the liver and heart, which chop fine, and mix with some good veal stuffing; fill the rabbit, and sew it up. Put two pounds of fat beef, and the same weight of pickled pork, into a saucepan with a quart of water and a good-sized onion sliced. Let them simmer slowly for an hour, then put in your rabbit, and boil all together for another hour. Skim off all the fat about ten minutes before serving, and thicken the gravy with flour and butter. Season with pepper and salt, and add a bunch of parsley boiled soft, and green and finely chopped. Lay the rabbit and the meat in a hot dish, and pour the sauce over.

23. *Stewed Rabbits.*—Clean the rabbits thoroughly, cut them up, and scald them for a short time; put some sliced onions and a bit of dripping into your pot, and fry the rabbits with them till slightly browned, dredge in a little flour, then add hot water sufficient to make gravy, pepper and salt, and a little catsup. Stew them very gently for an hour.

24. *Irish Stew.*—Put two pounds of breast of mutton into a pot, with a pint and a half of water and a pinch of salt; let it stew gently for an hour; then take off all the fat; take out the meat and cut it into small pieces; have ready four pounds of potatoes, pared and cut in halves; three or four good-sized onions, peeled and sliced; and pepper and salt, mixed in a cup. When you have taken the fat off the broth as closely as possible, put in a layer of potatoes; then sprinkle two or three pieces of meat with the pep-

per and salt, and lay them on the potatoes, then a layer of the sliced onions, then another layer of potatoes, one of mutton, then one of onions, and so on till the whole is in. Cover close, and let it stew very gently for another hour, shaking it frequently, that it may not burn.

25. *To Dress Lamb's Head and Pluck.*—Wash the head thoroughly clean, and remove the brains; put the head, with the heart and part of the liver, into a saucepan, and cover it with water. Put in also a small onion, peeled, and a little salt; skim it often as it comes to the boil, and let it boil very gently for an hour and a quarter; take them out, and lay the head flat on the dish; put it before the fire to brown; put the brains, which have been thoroughly washed and picked, into the liquor, to boil, while you mince, very small, the heart and liver; then take out the brains and mince them also; dredge over them a tablespoonful of flour, and add a little chopped parsley, pepper and salt; put this back into the saucepan with as much of the broth as will make it a good thick sauce; boil it up two or three times, and pour it over the head. A few thin slices of bacon, fried and laid round the dish, is a great improvement.

26. *Haricot Mutton.*—Make a good gravy by boiling the rough bits and trimmings, seasoning it with pepper and salt and a little catsup. Strain, and add carrots, parsnips, onions, and celery, previously boiled tender; slice them in; then pepper and salt your mutton; broil it brown; put it into the gravy along with the vegetables; and stew all together for about ten minutes or a quarter of an hour. Garnish with small pickles.

27. *Bubble and Squeak.*—Cut cold boiled beef in slices about a third of an inch thick. Fry them till heated through, and of a light brown; keep them hot before the fire. Have ready chopped some cold boiled cabbage; fry this in the pan, stirring it well about, and season it with pepper and a very little salt. Put the cabbage into a dish, and lay the meat around it.

28. *To Prepare Sausage Meat.*—Take one-third fat, and two-thirds lean, of either pork or beef, chop it very fine, and to every twelve pounds of meat add twelve spoonfuls of pounded salt, six of ground pepper, and, if agreeable, nine spoonfuls of sifted sage, with a little dried winter savory rubbed to a powder. Mix well, and put the meat into skins, or make it into flat balls and fry them in hot fat.

Bologna sausages are made of veal, pork, and ham, in equal quantities, chopped fine and seasoned with sweet herbs and pepper, then put into skins, boiled till tender, and dried.

29. *Beefsteak Pudding*—Rub half a pound, of dripping or lard, or suet, into a pound and a half of flour, with a pinch of salt, and make it into a stiff paste with as little water as possible; then, having greased the inside of your basin, lay a thin crust over the same, except just the bottom, as it will else absorb all the gravy; now have ready some pieces of steak or beef-skirt, well seasoned with pepper and salt, put a piece of fat at the bottom, then lay in all your meat; after which pour in about a teacupful of broth or water, then moisten the edges of the crust round the basin, and lay on a cover of the remainder of the paste, pinching the two

edges together; dip your cloth into hot water, flour it well, and tie it tightly over the pudding. Put it into a saucepan of boiling water, make it boil up quickly, and keep it boiling from three to four hours.

TO DRESS VEGETABLES.

GENERAL DIRECTIONS.—Pick and wash greens thoroughly; pick them close, for an outside leaf will deteriorate a dishful; split the stems of cabbages across twice. They should be washed in a pan, as particles of sand or dust hang round wooden vessels; do not pour or pump the water on them, but plunge them in; throw into the water a good handful of salt, as that will draw out worms or other insects. which you cannot see without pulling the vegetables to pieces. All greens should be boiled by themselves, in plenty of water, with a good lump of salt; the water should boil when they are put in, and be kept boiling; they should be well done, or they are unwholesome; a very little bit of soda put into the water mellows the greens and preserves their color.

No directions can be given as to the time vegetables take for boiling; much depends on size and age. To ascertain when they are done, pass a fork through the stem; if soft, they are done; they begin to sink when nearly boiled enough. Greens should be perfectly strained immediately they are done.

30. *To Dress Potatoes.*—In general it will be found best to pare them before boiling; they should also be as nearly of a size as possible, or the small ones will break before the large ones are done; they should be put into cold water scarcely enough to cover them, with a good lump of salt; they should boil slowly, and when they begin to crack the water should be poured off; then set the saucepan over the fire with the lid off, till they are quite dry and mealy. On serving, cover them with a clean napkin.

31. *To Boil Green Peas.*—Peas should be boiled as soon as shelled. Put them into boiling water with a little salt; no soda, as that will break them. The time they will take depends on their age; in general about twenty minutes is enough. When done, strain them through a sieve and pour them into a vegetable dish over a good lump of butter. A few sprigs of green mint should be boiled and served up with the peas.

32. *To Boil Beans.*—After shelling, put them into boiling water with a handful of salt; they will be cooked in about half an hour; when the skins feel tender they are done enough; strain them, and serve them with parsley and butter.

33. *Haricot Beans.*—These are a very agreeable vegetable, and will be found a good substitute for potatoes when the latter are scarce and dear. They may be dressed in several ways. As they are the dried seeds of the French bean, they require soaking for several hours before they are fit to cook. Put them into cold water with salt in it, and let them simmer for three or four hours. As soon as they begin to crack, pour off the water and stand them on the hob to dry. They are eaten with the gravy of the meat like potatoes, unless preferred with melted butter.

34. *French or Scarlet Beans.*—Cut off the two ends and string them, then split and cut them in two, throw them into a pan of clean water, and put them into plenty of boiling water with some salt and a little bit of soda. When they are soft, which will be in about a quarter of an hour or twenty minutes, strain them through a sieve, and serve them with melted butter in a boat.

35. *To Boil Turnips.*—Pare your turnips pretty thick, split them and boil them in plenty of water, with salt in it, for about half an hour; try them with a fork; if tender, they are done; strain and serve them with a little melted butter in a boat, or mash them up with a little butter, pepper, and salt. They should be boiled by themselves.

36. *To Boil Carrots.*—Scrape and wash them, then split them in two, if very large, into four, and cut them across; they require long boiling to make them soft. *Parsnips* are dressed in the same manner. When cold they are very nice cut in slices and fried.

37. *To Boil Cabbages.*—Cut off the stalk, and strip off the outer leaves, quarter, and wash them in plenty of water, and leave them to soak, top downwards, with a little salt in the water, for an hour or two. Put them into plenty of boiling water, with a good handful of salt and a bit of soda, and boil them till the stalk feels tender. Cabbages require boiling from twenty to forty minutes, according to their age and size. Drain them through a colander. Greens may be pressed between two plates.

38. *To Dress Cauliflowers.*—Having picked it into small pieces, which is absolutely necessary in order to remove the slugs with which this vegetable abounds, wash it thoroughly in several waters, and let it lay to soak for full an hour before you dress it. Put it into a saucepan of boiling water with a lump of salt, and when tender it will be done; let it drain in a colander, and serve it up with melted butter. Some persons may prefer to see them brought to table whole; but they must then take the chance of being helped, along with the cauliflower, to some unsightly insect, which would be sufficient to disgust the least delicate stomach; besides, if properly boiled, and laid carefully in the dish, the pretty appearance of the vegetable is by no means destroyed by it having been divided.

39. *Broccoli Sprouts.*—Pick and wash them well, and boil them in plenty of water, with salt in it; when they are tender strain and let them cool; when cold, to heat them again, dredge them with flour, and fry them in butter, sprinkle them with a little salt, and serve them up.

40. *To Dress Spinach.*—It must be carefully picked, the yellow leaves removed, and the ends of the stalks cut off. It requires to be washed in four or five waters, as it is apt to be gritty. When quite clean lay it in a colander to drain. Put it into a saucepan of boiling water, with a large tablespoonful of salt. When it has boiled a few minutes strain the water off, and fill up again with boiling water, adding salt as above. Keep it boiling till quite tender, pressing it down frequently, that it may be done all alike. It will be done enough in about ten minutes or a quarter of an

DOMESTIC COOKERY.

hour. When done, squeeze it between two plates till thoroughly dry, lay it on a dish, and cut it quite through in small squares.

41. *Asparagus.*—Cut the heads about four or five inches long; scrape them and throw them into cold water; tie them in bundles; put them into boiling water with plenty of salt in it; let them come quickly to a boil—they will take from a quarter of an hour to twenty minutes. When tender take them up with a slice; drain them well; remove the string, and lay the asparagus in a dish, heads inwards, on slices of toast previously dipped in the liquor. Serve with melted butter. *Seakale* is dressed in the same manner.

42. *Beets.*—They must not be scraped or cut, as they would then lose their color and sweetness. Salt the water, and boil them for an hour, in summer, and in the winter for three hours. It makes a fine pickle if cut into slices when cold, and put into vinegar.

43. *Onions.*—Select the white kind, peel them, and put them into boiling milk, with a little salt, and let them boil from half an hour to three-quarters. Drain them through a colander and serve them with melted butter.

44. *Tomatoes.*—Pour scalding water over them to loosen the skins; thus let them remain for five minutes; then peel and put them into a stewpan, with a little salt and butter; stew them for half an hour; then pour them on buttered toast. Tomatoes are best cooked slowly.

45. *Vegetable Marrow.*—If large, cut them into quarters: otherwise they will not need it. Boil them till soft, then peel them—and some take out the seeds; lay them on buttered toast, and pour melted butter over them. They may be served in slices on toast, like asparagus, or mashed, like turnips, with butter, pepper and salt, and a little lemon peel.

46. *To Dress Mushrooms.*—Cut off the lower part of the stem, peel, and put them into a saucepan, with just enough water to keep them from burning: put in a little salt, and shake them occasionally. When tender flavor them with butter, pepper and salt; add wine and spice if agreeable. Serve on buttered toast.

47. *To Cook Rice.*—Pick, and wash it in cold water. To a pint of rice put three quarts of *boiling water* and a teaspoonful of salt. Let it boil just *seventeen minutes* from the time it fairly comes to a boil; then pour off *all* the water, and set it over a moderate fire with the saucepan uncovered; let it steam fifteen minutes. Accuracy with regard to time is very important.

48. *Artichokes.*—Boil them till tender, let them drain, and serve them with melted butter. They must be well washed and soaked before cooking.

49. *Jerusalem Artichokes.*—Scrape and wash them clean, and put them into boiling water with salt in it; large ones will require boiling for two hours. When done take them up and butter them.

50. *A Dressed Salad.*—Take small salad, lettuce, endive, celery, radishes, and young onions: pick and wash them quite clean, cut them up in small pieces, put them into a salad-bowl or deep dish, and pour over them the following dressing:—Bruise the yolk of a cold, hard-boiled egg with the back of a spoon on a plate, then pour on it about a teaspoonful of cold water and the same meas-

ure of salt; rub all together till it becomes smooth like a thick paste; add a teaspoonful of made mustard, and when this is well mixed also add and mix a tablespoonful of salad-oil or cold melted butter; after this add and mix two tablespoonfuls of vinegar. Ornament the top of the salad with small bits of the white of the egg and pickled beet-root alternately.

ROASTING MEAT.

GENERAL REMARKS.—In roasting meat it is necessary to have a good clear fire, in size according to your joint, to keep the joint constantly in motion, so that it may not scorch, but be cooked equally in every part, and to baste it frequently with its own dripping. When two-thirds done sprinkle it with salt. A screen should be placed round the fire to keep in the heat.

51. *To Roast Beef.*—Do not wash meat before putting it down to roast, as that will prevent its browning. Wipe it clean with a clean cloth, and hang it before the fire, which must act on all parts as uniformly as possible. The fire should be clear, free from all smoky coals in front, and of a strength according to what you have to roast. Do not place the meat too near at first, or you will have it browned on the outside before it is warm within. It is usual to allow a quarter of an hour to every pound of meat; but much of course will depend on the strength of the fire, and something also on the staleness or freshness of the meat. Fresh meat require more time to cook than that which is stale. When about half done sprinkle it with salt. A well-roasted joint should have a nice, rich brown tinge all over; and, in order to obtain this, attention to the fire, and careful, frequent basting, is indispensable, as well as judgment to remove it when it is sufficiently cooked. As it approaches the proper time the steam will be drawn towards the fire. When your joint is done lay it in a clean hot dish, pour off all the fat, and pour the nice brown gravy at the bottom of the dripping-pan over the meat, but no hot water, or you will infallibly spoil the flavor of both gravy and meat. Good meat will furnish sufficient gravy when cut. Garnish with scraped horseradish.

52. *To Roast Mutton.*—Mutton requires more cooking than beef, the latter being by many preferred somewhat underdone. A *shoulder* of mutton particularly, if it be not sufficiently roasted, has a strong woolly flavor; the fat tastes rancid, and is apt to spoil the appetite of a delicate stomach; if, on the contrary, it be nicely roasted brown, without being burned, and well basted, it is a delicious dish. Like beef, it must not be placed too near the fire at first, but must be suffered to become gradually hot through, and kept constantly turned. When you think it is about half done sprinkle a good bit of salt all over it, which is the general rule for all roasted meat. When it is done pour away the whole of the fat, and what little gravy remains at the bottom of the dish may be served up with the mutton. If it be good meat, the gravy will follow the knife as it is cut. Serve it up with onion-sauce.

A *leg* of mutton is roasted in the same manner, except that, being a much leaner joint, and the fat of a milder nature, it does not require so much cooking. The same may be said of the *loin* and the *best end of the neck*, care being taken to cut off the fat sufficiently close before roasting.

53. *To Roast Venison.*—Venison is roasted in the same way as mutton, only it requires more time. Cover it with buttered paper and paste before you set it down to roast; otherwise, it being such a dry sort of meat, and the little fat there is being so easily melted, the fire will draw out all the juices, and it will prove dry and tasteless. Baste it constantly, and serve it with a good gravy and currant jelly.

54. *To Roast Lamb.*—Lamb requires to be well roasted, as if not sufficiently done, it will fail to acquire that delicate taste so peculiar to it. It is commonly dressed in quarters. Lamb should be well jointed, or chopped by the butcher, as it is such a delicate sort of meat that it becomes altogether disfigured if the carver is compelled to hack and pull it in pieces. In roasting, baste with its own dripping, and, after pouring off all the fat, serve it up in a hot dish with the gravy that remains after the fat is poured off. In serving up a fore-quarter, the cook should divide the shoulder neatly from the ribs, and, after squeezing the juice of half a lemon on the ribs cover the shoulder closely over again. It is usual to send up with lamb mint-sauce in a tureen.

55. *To Roast Veal.*—All parts of veal are good roasted, excepting the scrag end of the neck, which is commonly used for stewing or making pies. Roast veal is much improved by a stuffing composed of chopped suet and parsley, lemon-peel, a little thyme, savory, marjoram, a little grated nutmeg and bread-crumbs, seasoned with pepper and salt, all mixed together with an egg. The bones should be carefully taken out, and the stuffing put in their place; then cover your veal with buttered paper to prevent it burning, and set it down before a strong, clear fire, not too close at first, as it requires more dressing than beef or mutton, it being extremely unwholesome if underdone. When nearly enough roasted, take off the paper and let it brown; sprinkle it with salt, and baste it well either with its own dripping, or, if there be not enough, with lamb dripping or butter. Pour melted butter over it before sending it to table. Garnish with lemon cut in quarters or sliced.

56. *To Roast Pork.*—Pork should at all times be perfectly well done, and therefore requires a longer time to roast than any other meat. Pork is much more savory when stuffed with chopped sage and onions and bread-crumbs, seasoned with pepper and salt. The outer rind should be neatly scored, to enable the carver to cut slices more easily. Before setting it down to roast, rub the skin with salad-oil to prevent its blistering, and baste it frequently. Serve it with apple-sauce in a tureen or boat. The onions should be boiled a little before being chopped for the stuffing.

57. *To Roast Sucking Pig.*—When the pig is properly prepared and cleaned by the butcher, cut off the feet, and making a stuffing of chopped sage, crumbs of bread, butter, pepper, and salt, according to your taste and judgment, but let the bread be the principal ingredient; fill the inside of the pig with the stuffing, and sew up the slit. Baste with butter. It will require from two

to three hours' roasting, according to the size. The skin should be nicely browned and crisp. Before sending it to table, split it down the back from head to tail, and lay it, with the skin side uppermost, flat in the dish. The head is cut off and a half laid at each end. Take out the brains, and having previously boiled the liver, chop it up with the brains, and mix them together with veal or beef gravy in a small tureen. Apple-sauce as for pork.

58. *To Roast Ox Heart.*—Having emptied out all the blood, wash it well and dry it with a clean cloth, cut off the deaf-ears, which lay to soak in a little lukewarm water. Fill all the openings of the heart with a good veal stuffing, and cover the top with a sheet of writing-paper to prevent scorching; suspend it with the pointed end downwards, and keep it well basted. It will require about two hours to roast, as it should be well done. When nearly roasted or done enough, take off the paper and let it brown. While the heart is roasting, put the deaf ears into a clean saucepan, with a little water, some salt, an onion, and a few allspice; let it stew gently, and keep it well skimmed. About a quarter of an hour before you serve up the heart, put a crust of bread nicely browned into your gravy, with a lump of butter rolled in flour; let it mix and boil up, then strain it through a sieve, and after skimming off all the fat from the dripping-pan, put the gravy that remains at the bottom, along with that which you have made, back into the gravy saucepan, and boil all together. Lay the heart in a very hot dish set over another filled with boiling water, pour a little of the gravy over it, and send up the remainder in a hot tureen. This is a very nice savory dish, but it chills so soon that the plates and dishes must be very hot; indeed, hot-water plates are always used by those who have them. Some persons boil the heart for a quarter of an hour before putting it down to roast, in order to prevent its chilling too soon.

What remains cold will be found extremely nice made into a hash the next day. It should be cut in thin slices with what stuffing there may be left, and warmed up with the gravy; a spoonful of catsup will be found a great improvement. Shake it well together, and pour it into a deep dish over thin snippets of toasted bread.

BOILING MEAT.

GENERAL DIRECTIONS.—Meat should be boiled in a vessel large enough to contain it easily, so that it may have perfect freedom and sufficient water, otherwise it will be hard and discolored; but too large a pot will leave unnecessary space, which ought to be avoided.

Before putting your joint into the pot, put in a plate turned upside-down, so that the water may get to every part, and the meat may not stick to the bottom. All kinds of meat should be put into cold soft water; and with fresh meat throw in a little salt to raise the scum. The water should not be suffered to come to a boil too quickly, and just before it boils the scum should be removed, and for a few minutes afterwards; for if the scum be suffered to boil down, it will render the meat black. When it is skimmed, quite clean, cover the pot and set it aside, so that it may only simmer, taking great care, however, that it never ceases to do so. Should the water waste in the boiling, it will be necessary to add more, so as to keep the meat covered; in this case boiling water must be used. If the meat be boiled in a cloth it will be whiter, but the liquor will be spoiled. It is usual to allow a quarter of an hour to every pound of meat, reckoning from the time the water begins to boil; but this is by no means an infallible rule, as some parts of meat require much more cooking than others. A piece of brisket of beef, for instance, requires much more time for cooking than a piece of the round of the same weight; and you would surely spoil the best end of the neck of mutton by boiling it the same length of time as the breast. The cook must use her own judgment on these matters. When meat is perfectly fresh it requires more time for cooking than when stale or long killed. Good meat invariably swells in boiling.

If corned meat be too salt, you may pour off the water after it has boiled a few minutes, and replace it with fresh.

59. *To Boil a Salted Round of Beef.*—Rinse it in a pan of cold water, cut out the bone, roll it round firmly, and bind it fast with a broad tape; put it into the pot and cover the lid close; keep it gently simmering, taking care to skim before it comes to a boil; allow a quarter of an hour to each pound of beef. The vegetables served with salt beef are carrots and greens, and sometimes turnips are added. When you dish it up, pour over the meat a very little of the liquor in which it has been boiled. Do not, if you can avoid it, boil any vegetables with the meat.

60. *To Boil an Aitch-bone of Beef.*—Follow the directions given for the round, only that a large one will take less time in proportion; for instance, one weighing twenty pounds will be done in rather less than four hours.

61. *To Boil a Piece of Brisket of Beef or Thin Flank.*—These are boiled in the same way as the round, only that they require much longer boiling, being of so close a texture, and the fat of such a peculiar nature, that, if not sufficiently cooked, the meat will be hard and spongy, and will taste extremely disagreeable; so much so that persons who have once partaken of those parts under-boiled will feel very unwilling to eat of them again. A piece of brisket or thin flank of beef, weighing eight pounds, will take four hours' boiling. To know if it be boiled enough, you may insert a fork through the meat a little way, and if it feel soft, then it is done. Peas-pudding is good with boiled beef. Brisket of beef if to be eaten cold, should be laid on a board, and a heavy weight should be set on it, to press out all the loose fat; it then cuts smooth and solid.

62. *To Boil a Leg of Mutton.*—If your pot be not long enough to let the leg lie straight, you may cut the tendon at the joint and bend round the shank. Do not put in too much water, as the liquor will make good broth. Throw a little salt into the water when you put in the mutton, as that will make the scum rise, which must be taken off clean. Let it boil slowly and equally. A good-sized leg of mutton, say of eight pounds, will be done suffi-

ciently in two hours. Do not boil turnips or any other vegetable with the meat, as they will flavor it, and prevent its keeping so well when cold. Dish it with a very little of the liquor, as if the meat be good, and not too much boiled, it will yield sufficient gravy when cut. Mashed turnips form the appropriate vegetable to this dish, with caper sauce.

63. *Neck of Mutton* is dressed the same as the leg. The *breast* requires more boiling and will take half an hour to the pound. Serve with parsley and butter.

64. *To Boil a Leg of Lamb.*—A leg of lamb is a delicate dish when nicely boiled. If whiteness is desirable, wrap it in a clean cloth; only the liquor will then be spoiled for broth. Boil one of five pounds gently for about an hour and a half. When you dish it cut the loin into chops, fry them, and lay round it. Sauce plain melted butter, or parsley and butter.

65. *To Boil a Leg of Veal.*—Take out the bone, and fill the space with a stuffing made of bread crumbs, minced salt pork, suet chopped fine, parsley, sweet herbs, pepper, salt; sew up the opening, or draw the flap over it, and skewer it down. Put it into a long pot, and cover it with cold water with a tablespoonful of salt; skim it well, and let it simmer slowly till done enough, which may be ascertained by passing a fork into it. Serve with parsley and butter, or oyster-sauce. The liquor will make excellent soup or broth with the addition of vegetables.

66. *To Boil a Knuckle of Veal.*—Break, or rather saw the knuckle into pieces; wash, and put it into plenty of water, with a little salt; let it boil gently for two or three hours, according to the size; it requires to be well boiled, in order to soften the sinews, which, when sufficiently done, are most delicious; you must keep it well skimmed, as the liquor is excellent for broth or soup. It is eaten with boiled ham, bacon, or pickled pork. When dished, pour over it some good parsley and butter.

67. *To Boil a Chump of Veal.*—Wrap the joint in a cloth in order to have it white and delicate; put it into a pot with a little salt and cover it with water; let it simmer gently for about an hour and a half after it comes to a boil. When done, fry some thin rashers of ham or bacon, lay them round it on the dish, and serve it up with oyster-sauce.

68. *To Boil a Calf's Head.*—Wash and cleanse the head thoroughly; take out the brains and soak them in cold water, and pick them quite clean. Boil the head slowly for an hour and a half; then put the brains into a small saucepan, and boil them in half a pint of the liquor for half an hour. Then take up the head in a dish, mash the brains and season them with pepper and salt: turn them back into the little saucepan, add a few bread-crumbs, a lump of butter rolled in flour, and a glass of wine; shake all well together, just give it a boil, and serve it for sauce, either poured over the head, or separately in a boat. The liquor will make ex⚫ cellent soup the next day.

69. *To Boil a Sheep's Head.*—Soak and wash the head well in cold water, taking care to remove all the splinters of the bones, and to clean the brains thoroughly of all the skin and blood. Put it into a saucepan, cover it with lukewarm water and a good spoonful of

DOMESTIC COOKERY.

salt; let it boil very gently, skimming it well from time to time. When it has boiled about an hour, take off all the fat; and having cut up a good-sized onion, two turnips, a carrot, a small head of celery, and a sprig or two of parsley, put them into the broth with a little thyme and a crust of bread toasted brown; cover up the saucepan, and let the broth simmer gently for an hour and a half, when the head will be done. Serve it up with the brains chopped up in melted butter, poured over it, and turnips in another dish. Serve the broth, which will be excellent, in a tureen.

70. *To Boil Pickled Pork.*—Having washed and scraped it, put it into boiling water with the skin side uppermost. If it be thin, a piece of four pounds will be done in less than an hour; a leg of eight pounds will take three hours. Pork should be done enough; but if boiled too fast or too long, it will become jelly. Keep the pot well skimmed, and send it to table with peas-pudding and greens.

71. *To Boil Bacon and Beans.*—These must be boiled separately, otherwise the bacon will spoil the color of the beans. Soak the bacon for an hour or two in cold water, trim and scrape it as clean as possible, and put it into enough cold water to cover it; set it over a slow fire, so that it will be half an hour before it comes to a boil; then skim it and let it boil gently till done. Two or three pounds will require an hour and a half after it boils; the hock or gammon, being thick, will require more time. When done enough, strip off the rind; and your beans in the meantime having been boiled and strained, put them into a deep dish, lay the bacon upon them, and send them to table, with parsley and butter in a boat.

72. *To Boil a Ham.*—If the ham has been long cured, soak it in cold water for from twelve to twenty hours. Scrape it and put it into a large vessel to boil with plenty of cold water, and let it simmer gently from three to four or five hours, according to the size. A ham of twenty pounds will require four hours and a half. Skim the pot frequently, to remove the grease as it rises. When done, strip off the rind, and stew bread raspings over the top side; then set it before the fire, or in the oven, to dry and brown. Some persons prefer to bake a ham; it is then necessary, after soaking and scraping, to inclose it in a paste of flour and water before sending it to the oven.

73. *To Boil a Tongue.*—Soak it all night before using, and be careful to wash out the salt, which is put into various crevices to preserve it. Boil it in plenty of water from two hours and a half to three hours. Remove the skin before sending it to table, and garnish with parsley.

74. *To Boil Tripe.*—Wash it clean and put it on to boil in plenty of water with four or six moderately sized onions. When the onions are quite soft the tripe will be boiled enough. Serve it with the onions in a hash-dish with a little of the liquor in which it has been boiled, and plain melted butter on a boat.

75. *To Boil Cow Heel.*—Cow heel should be boiled till the bones will slip out, with an onion and some salt in the water. Serve with parsley and butter.

FRYING.

GENERAL REMARKS.—In frying much depends on the pan being in good condition and perfectly clean. If it be thin, it soon becomes so hot that it either scorches the meat or sets the fat alight; and if it be not clean to a nicety, it discolors the meat and gives it a bad flavor. It should never be cleansed with anything but fat; washing it with water makes it rusty. After frying fish, turn the pan over the fire for a minute or two; this will destroy the smell and taste of the fish. The fire should be clear and brisk, not blazing, but strong.

Lard or dripping is best to use for frying in. To know if the fat be the right heat, throw in a bit of bread, which should fry a light brown. Shake the pan constantly while frying, to prevent the meat sticking or burning. Drain the fat off your fish or meat by laying them on a wire sieve.

76. *To Fry Sausages.*—Sausages require to be dressed very slowly. Before you put them into the pan prick them in several places with a fine fork, to prevent them bursting; put a lump of dripping into a clean frying-pan, and as soon as it is melted, but before it becomes hot, put in the sausages; shake the pan frequently, so that they may not stick; let them get hot very gradually, and brown them nicely all over. When done lay them on a hot dish before the fire.

77. *To Fry Liver and Bacon.*—Wash the liver, but do not soak it; dry it, and cut it in slices rather thin; then scrape your bacon, cut off the rind, and slice it very thin; make your pan hot, and fry the bacon quickly, and not too much; it will yield sufficient fat in which to fry the liver; lay the bacon in a hot dish before the fire, and fry the liver, which also should not be too much done, or it will be dry. When the liver is done enough lay it over the bacon, and pour into the pan half a cupful of flour and water with a little pepper, but no salt; stir it well about, and strain whatever fat or gravy may be in the dish, under the liver and bacon, into the pan, let it boil up, then pour it over the meat, or garnish with sliced lemon.

78. *To Fry Beefsteaks and Onions.*—Cut the steaks about three-quarters of an inch thick; put a good lump of dripping or lard into your pan, and when it is hot lay in the steaks; turn them frequently, so that they may not burn; let them be nicely browned all over, and, when cooked, lay them in a hot dish before the fire; meantime, have in readiness a plateful of onions, sliced very thin, and sprinkled with pepper and salt; put them into the pan, and lay a dish over them to keep in the steam; turn them about, and let them be cooked thoroughly. They will require a long time; they should be soft and brown; when done pour them over the steaks and serve up hot.

79. *To Fry Veal Cutlets.*—Veal cutlets should be fried either in veal dripping or butter. Cut them half an inch thick, beat up an egg, and with a whisk lay it over the cutlet on each side; after which dip it in bread-crumbs and lay it in the pan. Dress cutlets slowly and thoroughly, of a light brown. For gravy, take half a cupful of water thickened with flour, a lump of butter, a little pepper and salt, a pinch of sweet herbs rubbed fine, and a little

lemon-juice; mix all together and put into the pan; boil it up and pour it over the cutlets. It is usual to fry bacon or ham with veal cutlets, and to serve them in a separate dish. Lamb chops are fried in the same way.

80. *To Fry Pork Chops.*—Cut them rather thin, and cook them thoroughly. They are more savory if dipped in yolk of egg and strewed over with sage and onion finely chopped and mixed with bread-crumbs previous to frying.

81. *To Fry Bacon and Eggs.*—Cut the bacon in thin rashers and fry it as before directed; when done lay it in a hot dish before the fire. Break the eggs in separate cups and place them gently in the pan; keep them in a round flat shape. When the white is set take them out of the pan with a slice, and place an egg on each rasher.

82. *To Fry Tripe.*—Wash the tripe, and dry it well in a cloth. Cut it in long pieces about three inches wide. Make a thick batter of egg, flour, milk, a little minced onion, and a little salt. Dip the tripe into the batter and fry it in lard or good dripping, of which there must be sufficient in the pan almost to cover the tripe. Fry it of a light brown, and garnish with fried parsley.

83. *To Fry Parsley.*—Fried Parsley is used only for garnishing. It must be well dried first, and then fried in hot butter or dripping. Lay it on a sieve before the fire to drain the fat from it. In garnishing, place it round the edge of the dish.

BROILING.

GENERAL DIRECTIONS.—For broiling, the fire should be brisk and perfectly clear; a good strong cinder fire is best. Set the gridiron over for a minute or two to get hot, then wipe it quite clean with a clean damp cloth—do not use paper: then rub a bit of hard dripping or suet over the bars, to prevent the meat sticking to them. Put the lean of the meat on the back part of the gridiron, and the fat in the front; pepper your meat before you lay it on, but do not salt it, as that draws out the gravy. Turn the meat once or twice, but do not insert a fork for that purpose. Do not beat the meat before broiling; it will not make tough meat tender, and it expels the juices.

Broiled meat should be cooked quickly, and served quite hot; on taking it off the gridiron, lay it on a hot dish, sprinkle it with salt, and lay a good lump of butter over it. Some persons like catsup or walnut-liquor with broiled meat; others like the dish rubbed with a shallot.

84. *To Broil Beefsteaks.*—Beefsteaks, when properly broiled, form a dish which is generally liked. The gridiron should be thoroughly clean, not only on the tops of the bars, but on the sides also. Cut the steaks about three-quarters of an inch thick; dust them with pepper before laying them on the gridiron; they ought not to be turned too frequently; indeed, some persons turn them only once; this, however, depends greatly on the taste of those who are to partake of them; because, while some persons prefer them in a half-raw state, others like them well done. Rub a hot

dish with a shallot, place the steaks when cooked in the dish, and rub them over with a lump of butter, sprinkle them with salt, and serve them up hot. They should be eaten immediately; every moment they stand they become deteriorated in proportion. Either oyster-sauce or mushroom-sauce may be used when any is required.

85. *To Broil Mutton Chops.*—Mutton chops should not be broiled on too fierce a fire, otherwise the fat will cause the fire to flare, and the chops will be smoked and blackened. Pepper them the same as beefsteaks; but, unlike those, mutton chops require constant turning. They should not be overdone. When done enough, lay them in a hot dish and sprinkle with salt; they require no butter, the chops being sufficiently fat.

86. *To Broil Ham.*—Cut the ham about the third of an inch thick, and broil it very quickly over a brisk fire; lay it on a hot dish, pepper it, and put on it a good lump of butter.

87. *To Broil Pork Chops.*—These should not be cut quite so thick as mutton chops, and require more dressing: turn them frequently, and make them a nice light brown. When dished, sprinkle upon them a little sage powdered very fine.

88. *To Broil Kidneys.*—Split them through lengthways, and run an iron skewer through them to keep them flat; pepper them, and broil them over a clear fire. They should be lightly done. Serve them in a very hot dish, sprinkle them with salt, and put a bit of butter on each.

89. *To Boil Eggs.*—The best way is to put them into cold water; and when they have boiled up once or twice, if fresh, they will be done. Some persons prefer putting them into boiling water; they should then boil three minutes after they come to a boil.

90. *To Poach Eggs.*—Have a saucepan of water boiling, crack your eggs into separate cups, and put them, one at the time, into the water, taking a little into the cup before you turn the egg in; when the white has hardened round the yolk, which it will in a minute or two, take them out with a slice. They are delicious laid on rashers of fried bacon and ham.

91. *A very delicate Omelette.*—Beat six eggs, the yolks and whites separately; melt a bit of butter in a teacupful of warm milk, to which add gradually a teaspoonful of flour, a tablespoonful of salt, and a little pepper; then mix in the yolks of the eggs, and lastly the whites, beaten to a stiff froth. Bake immediately in a flat pan. Some ham cut fine and added is a great improvement; some persons like sweet herbs; others prefer some finely shred onion.

92. *Eggs and Spinach.*—This forms a pretty dish for supper. Having boiled and prepared some spinach (see *Vegetables*), poach some eggs, trim, and lay them on the spinach.

SAUCES.

As sauces spoil by standing long after they are made, they should be prepared last, and served hot.

93. *Melted Butter.*—Put a tablespoonful of flour into a clean

saucepan, mix it carefully with a little water at a time, till you have about a cupful; now cut into it, in small pieces four ounces of butter, shake it rapidly round till well mixed, then place it on the fire, watch it constantly, and keep shaking and turning it round until it boils; it is then ready. Be careful to turn it always one way, or the butter will oil. Should this happen, you may recover it in some measure by putting into it a little cold water and pouring it backwards and forwards several times. For fish, some salt should be added, and a little pepper.

94. *Onion Sauce.*—Peel the onions and boil them in plenty of water till they are perfectly soft; then strain them from the water and chop them very fine, season them with pepper and salt, and stir them into melted butter. Some persons add a little milk, which makes the sauce both rich and white.

95. *Egg Sauce.*—Boil the eggs till they are quite hard. Peel and chop them fine, season with pepper and salt, and stir them into melted butter.

96. *Bread Sauce.*—Crumble some stale bread very fine, set it on the fire in a saucepan, with as much sweet milk as will make it thick, put in a slice of onion, and stir it till the bread is soaked and the sauce is quite smooth. Season with pepper and salt.

97. *Mushroom Sauce.*—Pick out the stems, skin them, and the mushrooms also. Cut them up small, and wash them; put them into a saucepan, cover them with water, and let them stew gently till they are soft, when they will yield a fine rich gravy; then stir in a lump of butter kneaded into some flour to thicken it, and season with pepper and salt.

98. *Mint Sauce.*—Pick off the leaves of fresh green mint; wash them, then chop very fine, mix up some vinegar and sugar, and stir in the mint.

99. *Oyster Sauce.*—Simmer the oysters in their own liquor till they are plump; strain off the liquor through a sieve, wash the oysters clean, and beard them; put them into a saucepan, and pour the liquor over them, taking care you do not pour in any of the sediment; add a blade of mace, a quarter of a lemon, a spoonful of anchovy-liquor, and a bit of horseradish; boil it up gently, then take out the horseradish, the mace, and the lemon, the juice of which must be squeezed into the sauce. Now add some thick melted butter, toss it together, and boil it up.

100. *Anchovy Sauce, for Fish.*—Take a little good gravy, and anchovy, a quarter of a pound of butter rolled in flour, and stir all together till it boils. You may add a little lemon juice, catsup, red wine, or walnut-liquor, according to your taste. Some add cream.

101. *Lobster Sauce.*—Take a fine hen lobster; when boiled, take out all the spawn and bruise it in a mortar very fine, with a little butter; take all the meat out of the tail and claws, cut it in small square pieces, and put it aside. Put into a saucepan a spoonful of anchovy-liquor, a spoonful of catsup, a blade of mace, a bit of horseradish, half a lemon, a gill of gravy, a little butter rolled in flour, just enough to thicken it, and half a pound of butter nicely melted. Boil it gently up for six or seven minutes; then take out the horseradish, mace, and lemon, squeezing the juice of the latter

into the sauce; just simmer it up; then put in your lobster and spawn, and allow it to get hot through.

102. *Shrimp Sauce.*—Take a half a pint of shrimps, pick and lay them aside; put the pickings into a little water, stew it a short time, then strain off the liquor, with which make your melted butter; put in your shrimps, add a spoonful of anchovy-liquor and a little lemon-juice, and let it simmer altogether for a few minutes.

103. *A good Common Sauce for Fish.*—Plain butter melted thick, with a spoonful of walnut-pickle or mushroom-catsup.

104. *Sweet Sauce.*—Plain melted butter, sweetened with sugar to your taste.

105. *Caudle Sauce for Plum Pudding.*—Make melted butter, and stir it into a glass of sherry, half a glass of brandy or rum, a little sugar, grated lemon-peel and nutmeg. Shake the saucepan round, but do not let it boil after you have added the spirits.

106. *Apple Sauce.*—Pare your apples, cut them in quarters and core them, put them into a saucepan with a very little water, let them boil till perfectly soft, then strain the liquor off, and mash the apples with a spoon; add two or three cloves, or a little bit of cinnamon, a bit of butter, a little grated lemon-pell, and sugar to your taste; mix all together, and set the saucepan on the hob for a few minutes.

107. *Celery Sauce for Fowls and Game.*—Take a large bunch of celery, wash and pare it clean, cut it in small thin pieces, and boil it gently in a little water till tender; then add some beaten mace, nutmeg, pepper, and salt, thicken with a piece of butter rolled in flour, then boil it up, and pour it into a dish.

You may make it with cream, thus: boil celery as before directed, and add mace, nutmeg, a piece of butter the size of a walnut, rolled in flour, and half a pint of cream; boil all together.

108. *Parsley and Butter.*—Pick and wash a handful of parsley, tie it up, and throw it into boiling water for a minute or two; then cut away the stalks and chop the parsley very small; make melted butter, and stir in the parsley.

109. *Wine Sauce for Mutton or Venison.*—Take a sufficient quantity of the liquor in which the meat was boiled, put in pepper, salt, currant-jelly, and wine to your taste; boil all up, and thicken it with scorched flour mixed with a little water.

110. *Mushroom Sauce for Boiled Fowls.*—Stir half a pint of cream and a quarter of a pound of butter together one way, till it becomes thick; then add a spoonful of mushroom pickle, pickled mushrooms, or fresh. Garnish with lemon.

111. *Caper Sauce.*—Chop capers, and stir them into melted butter, adding some of the vinegar.

TO DRESS POULTRY AND GAME.

112. *To Roast Fowls.*—Pick and draw them; be careful not to break the gall-bag in drawing, as, if the gall be spilled, it will render any part which it touches bitter; a fowl should be so cleanly drawn as to require no washing, but merely to be wiped out with a clean dry cloth. Singe them; then press down the breast-

bone. Break the legs by the middle of the first joint, draw out the sinews, and cut off the parts at the break. Put the gizzard in one pinion and the liver in the other, and turn the points on the back; put a skewer in the first joint of the pinion and bring the middle of the leg close to it; put the skewer through the middle of the leg and through the body, and the same on the other side; put another skewer through the small of the leg and the sides- man, and another through the other side. Cut the head off close to the body, leaving sufficient skin to tie on the back. Suspend it neck downwards. Baste with butter for some time after put- ting to the fire. They will require from half an hour to an hour according to the size. When fowls are large they are very good stuffed like turkey.

Serve roast fowls with melted butter or gravy-sauce. Before you send them to the table, remove all skewers and strings which may have been used in trussing. Fowls and all other feathered animals are served with the breast upwards.

113. *To Roast a Turkey.*—Having picked, drawn, and singed the turkey, truss it according to previous directions for trussing fowls. Stuff the breast with rich veal stuffing, adding a little sausage-meat; sew up the neck. Cover the breast with buttered paper, to preserve it from scorching, and roast it to a fine brown. Baste it well with butter, and a little while before it is done re- move the paper and allow the breast to brown. A good-sized turkey will require roasting from an hour and a half to two hours. You must have plenty of good gravy in the dish, and garnish with lemon. Serve with bread-sauce.

114. *To Roast a Goose.*—Having picked, drawn, and singed the goose, cut off the head and neck, leaving sufficient skin to tie over the neck-bone. Take off the legs and wings at the first joint. Stuff with chopped sage and onion, and a few bread-crumbs sea- soned with pepper and salt. Cut off the end of the vent, and make a slit sufficiently large to admit the rump through, in order to keep the stuffing in. Tie the skin of the neck securely, to pre- vent the gravy from running out, and tie a string round the goose over the wings, and another over the legs. Paper the breast for a short time. Rub a few pieces of butter in the shoul- ders and back, to baste with; but, as it is naturally greasy, it will soon yield sufficient fat for that purpose. It will require full two hours' roasting. It should be well done. Serve it with plenty of gravy and apple-sauce. The liver, gizzard, head, neck, feet and pinions of the goose form what is termed the *giblets*, and make an excellent pie, or a savory stew, thus:

115. *Stewed Giblets.*—Having scalded and picked them, cut them in pieces, wash them clean, and put them into a saucepan with a piece of scrag of veal, cover them with water, and let them boil up; then take off the scum quite clean, and add three onions, two turnips, one carrot, and a little thyme and parsley. Stew them till they are tender, and strain them through a sieve; wash the giblets clean from the herbs, etc. Now take a piece of butter the size of a walnut, put it into a saucepan with a large spoonful of flour, and stir it about till it is well mixed and smooth; then put in the broth and giblets, stew them for a quarter of an hour,

season with salt and a little pepper, and just before you serve them up, chop a handful of green parsley, and put it in. Give it a boil up, and serve them in a tureen.

116. *To Roast Ducks.*—Pick, draw, and singe them. Cut off the head; dip the feet in boiling water to remove the yellow skin; truss them plump, turning the feet flat upon the back. Stuff the same as goose, and serve with gravy and apple-sauce. An hour will roast a duck. Green peas usually accompany roast duck.

117. *To Roast Pigeons.*—Pick, draw, and truss them, keeping on the feet. Chop the liver with some parsley, add crumbs of bread, pepper, salt, and a little butter; put this stuffing inside. Slit one of the legs, and slip the other through it; skewer and roast them for half an hour; baste them well with butter. Serve with brown gravy in a boat, and bread-sauce.

118. *To Roast Pheasants.*—Pick, singe, and draw them, the same as fowls. Truss them by twisting the head round one of the wings, and turning both wings on the back. Fix the legs down straight, the same as a roast fowl; the feet are to be left on. Paper them all over the breast, and roast them to a fine brown. Just before they are done, remove the paper and brown the breast; flour and baste them with a little butter, and let them have a fine white froth. They will be done in three-quarters of an hour. Take them up and pour good gravy into the dish. Serve with bread-sauce.

119. *To Roast Partridges.*—Pick, draw, singe, and clean them the same as fowls. Make a slit in the neck and draw out the craw; twist the neck round the wing, and bring the head round to the side of the breast. The legs and wings are trussed the same as fowls, only the feet are left on and crossed over one another. Put them down to a clear fire, and baste well with butter. When about half done, dust a little flour over them; let them be nicely browned. They will require to roast from twenty minutes to half an hour each. Serve on toasted bread dipped in the gravy, with gravy and bread-sauce.

120. *Grouse and Blackcock* should be dressed and served in the same manner, only the head should be trussed under the wing.

121. *To Roast Snipes or Woodcocks.*—These are not drawn. Spit them on a small bird-spit, flour and baste them with a piece of butter, lay a slice of bread toasted brown in the dish, and set it under the snipes for the trail to drop on. When they are done enough take them up and lay them on a toast. Have ready, for two snipes, a quarter of a pint of good gravy and butter; pour it into a dish, and set it over a chafing-dish for a few minutes. Garnish with lemon.

122. *To Roast a Hare.*—Cut off the feet and draw off the skin, commencing at the hind legs, and proceeding along the body to the head, taking care not to tear the ears in skinning them. Soak it well and wash it in several waters; then wipe it quite dry; make a stuffing with crumbs of bread, parsley, and beef suet chopped fine, a little grated lemon-peel and nutmeg, a piece of the liver boiled and chopped fine, and pepper and salt; moisten the whole with an egg, a little milk, and a spoonful of catsup. Put this pudding into the belly, and sew up the skin. Commence

trussing by placing the hind and fore legs flat against the sides. The under-sinews must be cut to make the hind legs lie flat. The head must be fixed between the shoulders on the back by running a skewer through it into the body. Suspend it head downwards. Baste it with butter, flouring it lightly. It will require from an hour and a half to two hours. The hare is served lying on its belly, with rich beef gravy and a dish of currant-jelly.

123. *To Roast a Rabbit.*—Having drawn and skinned it, wash it in warm water, dry it, truss it, and stuff it as follows: Beef suet chopped fine; a few bread-crumbs; a little thyme, marjoram, and savory; a little grated lemon-peel, pepper, and salt, mixed together with an egg; put it into the belly of the rabbit and sew it up. Suspend it before a good fire, and do not put it too close at first; baste it well with butter or veal dripping, and dredge it two or three times with flour. When it is sufficiently roasted place the rabbit in a hot dish; put a little water into a saucepan, a lump of butter rolled in flour, and pour the gravy in from the dripping-pan; give it a boil up, and pour it over the rabbit.

124. *A Batter for Roast Hare.*—Make a batter as for pancakes, but not quite so thick, with two spoonfuls of flour and two of salad-oil; add three yolks and one white of egg; mix all together with new milk and a little salt; baste the hare with it when half roasted.

125. *To Jug a Hare.*—Skin, draw, and wash the hare; cut it into pieces and put them into a jar with an onion, a bunch of sweet herbs, and a little water. Cover the top of the jar close, so that very little of the steam can escape; place the jar in a saucepan of water not sufficiently high to cover the top; keep the water constantly boiling between three and four hours. When done, skim off the fat, thicken the sauce with flour and butter; season with pepper and salt, and serve it all together in a hash-dish.

126. *To Boil a Turkey.*—A boiled turkey is a most delicate and excellent dish, and requires to be dressed with extreme care. Clean the turkey from feathers and stumps, and singe off the hairs, taking care not to blacken the skin. Draw and wipe it inside with a clean dry cloth; cut off the legs at the first joint; draw out the sinews; then pull down the skin and push the legs inside; cut the head off close to the body, leaving the skin long, and draw out the craw. Make a good veal stuffing and put it into the breast, leaving sufficient room for the stuffing to swell; then draw the skin of the breast over the opening and sew it neatly across the back, so that when the turkey is brought to table no sewing will appear. Place the gizzard in one wing and the liver in the other, turn the wings on the back and fix them to the sides with a skewer; wrap it in a cloth dredged with flour, and put it into a pot of warm water, in sufficient quantity to keep the turkey always covered. Skim it while boiling. A small, young turkey will not take more than an hour and a half to boil it; a large one about two hours and a half. When done place it in a hot dish, and pour a little sauce over the breast. Send up oyster-sauce, or parsley and butter, in a tureen. Some cooks make the stuffing of chopped bread and butter, oysters, cream, and the yolks of eggs.

127. *To Boil a Fowl.*—A fowl is prepared for boiling just the

same as a turkey, only omit the stuffing. It may be boiled without a cloth; the liquor will then be good. A small fowl will require from half an hour to three-quarters, a large one from an hour to an hour and a half. Sauce, parsley and butter.

128. *To Boil Rabbits.*—Wash them well in warm water; truss them like roast hare, and boil them for an hour; pour over them a sauce made of boiled onions chopped in melted butter, seasoned with pepper and salt, adding a little milk or cream.

129. *To Boil Pigeons.*—Boil them by themselves for a quarter of an hour; then boil a handsome square piece of bacon, and lay it in the middle of the dish; stew spinach to lay round, and put the pigeons on the spinach. Garnish with slices of bacon, and send up melted butter in a boat.

TO DRESS FISH.

GENERAL REMARKS.—Fish must be put into cold or boiling water according to its firmness of flesh: for instance, turbot salmon, mackerel, &c., should be put into cold water; while plaice, whitings, haddocks, and such soft-fleshed as well as crimped fish, should be put into boiling water. The reason is obvious: by putting flaccid and watery fish into the water cold, it is rendered still more soft and watery; but the boiling water sets it and renders it firmer; on the other hand, the cold water penetrates and softens the fish that is of a firmer texture, and makes it eat more tender and delicate. Keep the water skimmed while the fish is boiling.

Fish is cooked enough when it leaves the bone easily. Be sure to wash and clean your fish well, never trusting to the fishmonger.

In frying fish, having washed it, dry it thoroughly in a clean cloth, then flour it well, or whisk it over with egg, and dip it into bread-crumbs before frying it. Be sure your pan is very clean, and that your fat (of which there should be enough to cover the fish) boils before you put the fish in. Fry fish quickly of a fine light brown. Some like fish fried in batter—as good a batter as any is a little ale and flour beaten up just as you are ready for it—then dip the fish in before frying it. Put plenty of salt in the water in which you boil fish, and a stick of horseradish excepting mackerel, with which you boil salt, mint, parsley, and fennel.

130. *To Boil Turbot.*—Lay it in plenty of salt and water for an hour. In the meantime set on a fish-kettle with spring water and salt, and a piece of horseradish. Lay the turbot on a fish-plate, with the belly upwards, and put it in the kettle; let it be well boiled through, but not overdone; it will require from half an hour to three-quarters after it boils; according to the thickness. It should boil slowly. When it is done enough, take off the fish-kettle; set it before the fire, then carefully lift up the fish-plate, and set it across the kettle to drain; during which, melt a great deal of fresh butter, and bruise in the spawn of one or two lobsters, and the meat cut small, with a spoonful of anchovy-

liquor, then give it a boil and pour it into boats. Now lay the turbot in the dish, and garnish with scraped horseradish and lemon.

131. *To Boil Salmon.*—Clean out and scale the fish, and rinse it in water. Then put on a good roomy fish-kettle with plenty of water and a good handful of salt; put in your fish, let it boil very gently, keeping it skimmed. The time it will take depends greatly on the thickness of the fish. It is usual to reckon ten minutes to the pound. To ascertain if it be boiled enough, raise one end from the water, and if a knife pass easily betwixt the fish and the bone, it is sufficiently done. When it is ready, lift the drainer out of the water and set it across the kettle, that the water may drip from the fish. Serve it on a dish with a fish-plate; lay a napkin under the fish. Garnish with green parsley and lobster or shrimp sauce.

132. *To Boil Cod.*—wash and clean it well, boil it the same as directed for turbot. Serve it on a napkin. Garnish with parsley and horseradish scraped. Oyster-sauce.

133. *To Dress a Cod's Head and Shoulders.*—Clean a cod's head and shoulders in one piece, and lay it in salt all night. Before you dress it, bind it firmly together with tape. Put it into a fish-kettle with plenty of cold water, a handful of salt, and a stick of horseradish. Let it boil slowly for about three-quarters of an hour, then let the water drain from it across the top of the kettle. Place it on a hot dish, back upwards, and draw away the tapes very carefully. Brush it over with beaten egg and stew over it bread-crumbs, pepper and salt; then stick pieces of butter thickly over the top. Set it before the fire, which should be clear and brisk, to brown. Make a rich oyster-sauce with gravy well seasoned with cayenne pepper, salt, and catsup, and pour it into the dish, around but not over the fish.

134. *To Stew Cod.*—Cut it in slices an inch thick, lay them in a large stewpan, season with nutmeg beaten, pepper, and salt, a bundle of sweet herbs, an onion, half a pint of wine, and a quarter of a pint of water; cover close, and let it simmer softly for five or six minutes; then squeeze in the juice of a lemon, put in a few oysters, and the liquor strained, with a blade or two of mace; cover it close and let it stew softly, shaking the pan often. When it is done enough take out the sweet herbs and onion, and dish it up; pour the sauce over it, and garnish with lemon.

135. *To Boil Shell-Fish.*—Lobsters and craw-fish must be put alive in boiling water. When the joints come off easily they are done enough.

Crabs must be first killed, and then put into boiling water.

136. *To Fry Haddocks.*—These are most excellent fish when properly dressed. Take good-sized haddocks; wash and clean them well; let them lie all night in salt. When you are going to dress them, wash and wipe them dry; cut off the head, tail, and fins; skin them carefully, so as not to tear the flesh, which is extremely tender; cut the flesh from the bone and divide each side in two pieces; dredge them with flour, dip them in egg and bread-crumbs, and fry them in hot lard or dripping sufficient to cover them. Do not suffer the fat to scorch the fish. Brown both

sides; and when done, place them for a few minutes on a drainer, before the fire. Garnish with parsley. Send up oyster-sauce, or plain melted butter, in a boat.

137. *To Broil Haddocks.*—Scale, gut, and wash them clean. Do not rip open the bellies, but take out the guts with the gills; dry them in a clean cloth; and if there be any roe or liver, take it out, wash and dry it, and put it in again; flour them well, and have a clear, brisk fire. Clean your gridiron and let it get hot; then lay on your fish; turn them two or three times at first to keep them from sticking; then let one side be done enough, and turn it on the other. When done, lay them in a dish, and serve them with plain melted butter or anchovy-sauce. They are nice eating if salted a day or two before you dress them, and hung up to dry, or plain-boiled with egg-sauce.

138. *To Cook Dried Haddock.*—Take a frying pan or sauce-pan, and fill it with sufficient water to cover the haddock, and directly the water boils, place the fish in it for two or three minutes, according to its size. The haddock should then be skinned, buttered, and placed before the fire for a few minutes, when it is ready to serve.

139. *Baked Fish.*—Cod, gurnet, and shad are good for baking. Stuff them with a seasoning made of bread-crumbs, butter, salt, pepper, and (if agreeable) parsley and spices. Put the fish in a baking-dish, with a cupful of water and a lump of butter. Bake from three quarters of an hour to an hour.

140. *To Broil Mackerel.*—Cut off the heads, but do not rip them open; gut, and wash them clean, and dry them; pull out the roe at the neck end, boil it, then bruise it with a spoon; beat up the yolk of an egg with a little nutmeg, a little dropped lemon-peel, a little thyme, some boiled parsley chopped fine, a little pepper and salt, and a few bread-crumbs; mix these together with the mashed roe, and fill the mackerel; flour it, and broil it nicely. Send it up with a little catsup or walnut-pickle, in plain melted butter. Mackerel, if boiled, should be put into cold water with plenty of salt. When cold they are nice soused in vinegar.

141. *To Dress Flat-fish.*—In dressing all sorts of flat-fish take great care, if you *boil* them, to have them done enough, but do not let them break. Put plenty of salt in the water, also horseradish; let the fish be well drained, and cut off the fins when cleaning them. When to be fried, let them be well dried in a cloth; egg and bread-crumb them, and fry them of a light brown; use plenty of fat; and, when done, drain the fish on a clean coarse cloth. If to be fried without egg and bread-crumbs, proceed as for sausages.

142. *To Broil Herrings.*—Scale and gut them; cut off the heads; wash them clean, and dry them in a cloth; flour and broil them; mash the heads; boil them in small beer or ale, with a little whole pepper and an onion; let it boil for a quarter of an hour; strain it; then thicken it with butter and flour and a good deal of mustard. Lay the herrings on a dish and pour the sauce into a boat.

143. *To Fry Herrings.*—Gut and wash them clean, and dry them in a cloth; fry them brown; have ready some onions sliced

DOMESTIC COOKERY.

thin; fry them of a light brown, with the herrings; lay the herrings in a dish, and the onions round, with butter and mustard in a cup. Dress them on a quick fire.

144. *To Stew Eels.*—Clean them thoroughly, which will take plenty of water, time, and trouble; cut them in pieces of about three inches in length; put them into a saucepan with barely suf- ficient water to cover them, a blade or two of mace, and a crust of bread; let them stew gently till the flesh will strip easily from the bone; then put in a lump of butter rolled in flour, some pars- ley chopped fine, and a little pepper and salt; let it boil up once or twice, and serve them hot in a tureen with toasted snippets.

145. *To Broil Eels.*—Take a large eel; skin and make it clean; then open the belly, and cut it into four pieces. Then take the tail-end, strip off the flesh, and beat it in a mortar; season with a little beaten mace, grated nutmeg, pepper and salt, chopped pars- ley, thyme, lemon peel, and bread-crumbs; roll it in a piece of butter; then mix it again with the yolk of an egg; roll it up, and fill the pieces of belly with it; now cut the skin of the eel, wrap it round the pieces, and sew them up; broil them well; have butter and an anchovy for sauce, with the juice of a lemon.

146. *To Boil Soles.*—Take three quarts of spring-water and a handful of salt. When it boils put in the soles, and let them boil gently for ten minutes. Dish them up in a clean napkin, with anchovy or shrimp sauce.

147. *To Fry Soles.*—Scrape, but do not skin them; wash them and wipe them dry; dip them in beaten egg, and then strew them over with bread-crumbs; have a pan of fat, and be sure it boils before you put in the soles. Fry them of a light brown and turn them but once. Lay them on a napkin for the fat to drain off, and serve them on a fish-plate, with plain melted butter in a boat.

148. *To Stew Mussels.*—Wash them very clean from the sand, in two or three waters, put them into a saucepan, cover them close, and let them stew till all the shells open; then take them out, pick them out of the shells, and pick out the bit of weed which is usually sticking under the tongue. When you have picked them all clean put them into a clean saucepan, and to a quart of mussels strain half a pint of the liquor through a sieve; then put in a blade or two of mace, and a piece of butter, the size of a walnut, rolled in flour. Let them stew; then toast some bread, cut it in three- cornered pieces, and lay it round the dish. Pour in the mussels, and send them to table hot.

149. *To Scollop Oysters.*—Rub some bread-crumbs in a clean cloth; fill your scollop-shells with oysters and the bread-crumbs alternately. Set them before a good fire to brown, add a little pepper and salt, baste them well with butter, and keep turning them, that they may be brown all over alike.

150. *To Dress Salt Fish.*—Soak it for some hours, to take out the salt, changing the water frequently. Put it into cold water. It will take from ten to twenty minutes after it boils, according to the thickness of the fish. Serve it with boiled parsnips, and egg-sauce in a boat.

PIES AND PUDDINGS.

GENERAL RULES.—In boiling puddings mind that the cloth be perfectly clean. Dip it in hot water, and dredge it well with flour. If a bread pudding, tie it loose; if a batter-pudding, tie it nearly close; apple and gooseberry puddings, &c., should be tied quite close. When you make a batter pudding first mix the flour well with milk, and stir in the other ingredients by degrees; you will then have it smooth, without lumps. The best way, however, for a plain batter-pudding, is to strain it through a coarse hair-sieve, that it may have neither lumps nor the treadings of the eggs; and for all other puddings strain the eggs when they are beaten up. Be sure the water boils when you put your pudding in, and that it keeps boiling all the time, and that you keep it always covered with water; you should also move it about two or three times at first, or it may stick to the pot; dip the pudding into cold water immediately you take it out, which prevents it sticking. If you boil your pudding in a dish or basin, butter the inside before putting the pudding in; the same should be done to the dish for a baked pudding or pie.

The quality of pie crust depends much on the baking. If the oven be too hot, the paste, besides being burned, will fall; if too slack, it will be soddened, and consequently heavy.

Paste should be made on a cold, smooth substance, such as marble or slate, with a light, cool hand. It should be made quickly; much handling makes it heavy. Great nicety is required in wetting the paste; too little moisture rendering it dry and crumbly, while too much makes it tough and heavy; and in either case the paste cannot be easily worked. Practice alone can produce perfection in this art.

Before commencing to make paste for pies or puddings it is necessary to place near at hand everything likely to be wanted, to inspect all the utensils, to prepare all the ingredients, and, though last, not least, to wash the hands and nails perfectly clean; for the hands are the best tools to make paste with.

Always use good sweet butter, dripping, or lard for pie or pudding crust. Some persons entertain the mistaken notion that butter which cannot be eaten on bread will do very well for paste; on the contrary, the baking or boiling of rancid fat increases the bad flavor. It is a good plan to wash the butter in clean spring-water before using it. Make two or three holes with a fork in the cover of your pies, that the steam may escape.

151. *Puff-paste.*—Rub a quarter of a pound of butter into half a quartern of flour very fine; make it up into a light paste, using as little cold water as you can work it up with: then roll it out about a quarter of an inch thick, put a layer of butter all over, sprinkle on a little flour, double it up and roll it out again; double and roll it out thus four or five times, using another half-pound of butter; then it will be fit for any pies or tarts that require puff-paste.

152. *Crust for Raised Pies.*—Boil a quarter of a pound of lard in half a pint of water. This will bind two pounds of flour, on which it must be poured boiling. When well mixed, knead it on the paste-board with your hands till it becomes stiff like dough.

Cut off a piece first to form the cover, and model the rest like a dish or basin to hold the meat. When you put on the cover, wet the edges and press them tightly together.

153. *Rhubarb, Gooseberry, Plum, and Currant Pie.*—Make a good crust; lay a little round the sides of the dish; throw some sugar on the bottom, and put in a little cup to suck in the juice; lay in the fruit, and put some more sugar at top; then put in a very little water; wet the top of the crust that goes round inside the dish; put on the cover, and pinch the edges together. Cut the rhubarb into lengths of two inches, but do not skin it; only trim it at top and bottom.

154. *Apple Pie.*—Make a puff-paste crust; lay some round the sides of the dish; pare and quarter the apples, and take out the cores; lay a row of apples thick at the bottom of the dish, with half the sugar you intend for the pie, a little minced lemon-peel, a little of the juice, and two or three cloves, or a little cinnamon; then the rest of the apples and sugar; squeeze in a little more lemon-juice, and have ready the peels and cores of the apples boiled with some sugar in very little water and strained; pour the liquor into the pie, and put on the upper crust. It should be baked very pale. Put no cup in the dish when you make apple-pie. The flavor of a quince will greatly improve it.

155.—*Open Tarts.*—Line your dishes with thin, light paste, fill in with preserved fruits or jam, and lay strips of paste across in squares or diamonds. A short time will bake them.

156. *Mince Pies.*—Take equal weights of tender roast beef, suet, currants, raisins, and apples which have been previously pared and cored, with half their weight of soft sugar, one ounce of powdered cinnamon, an equal quantity of candied orange and lemon peel and citron, a little salt, and twelve bitter almonds blanched and grated. Chop the meat and the suet separately; wash and pick the currants, stone the raisins and chop them with the peel; and having minced all the ingredients very fine, mix them together, adding a nutmeg grated and the juice of a lemon. A glass or two of wine or spirit greatly improves it. Line your dish or patty-pans with puff-paste; fill with the mince, cover and pinch the edges together. Bake half an hour. Many persons make the mince without meat.

157. *Christmas Pudding.*—Cover the bottom of a baking-dish with very thin slices of stale bread-and-butter, with the crust cut off; strew it over thickly with mincemeat, then put another layer of bread-and-butter, cover this again with mincemeat, and so on till your dish is full; pour a good thick custard over all, and bake it for an hour, or an hour and a half, according to the size.

158. *Pigeon Pie.*—Make a puff-paste crust; cover the dish; let the pigeons be very nicely picked and cleaned; season them with pepper and salt, and put a good piece of fresh butter with pepper and salt in their bellies; lay them in the dish, the necks, gizzards, livers, pinions and hearts, place between, with the yolk of a hard-boiled egg and a beefsteak in the middle; put in as much water as will almost fill the dish, lay on the top crust and bake it well. It is a great improvement to stuff the pigeons with forcemeat, very highly seasoned, and to lay forcemeat-balls round inside the dish.

159. *Meat and Potato Pie.*—Mash some potatoes with pepper and salt and milk, and line a baking-dish with the same; lay on slices of cold meat of any kind, with salt, pepper, butter, and catsup; lay on more potatoes, then more meat, then another layer of potatoes on the top. Bake it till it is quite hot through.

160. *Giblet Pie.*—Take two sets of giblets nicely cleaned, put all but the livers into a saucepan, with two quarts of water, twenty corns of whole pepper, three blades of mace, a large onion and a bunch of sweet herbs; cover close, and stew them till they are tender; then have a good crust ready, cover the dish, lay a fine rumpsteak at the bottom, seasoned with pepper and salt; lay in the giblets with the livers, and strain the liquor in which they were stewed: season it with pepper and salt and pour it into the pie; put on the top crust, and bake it an hour and a half.

161. *Eel Pie.*—Make a good crust; clean, gut and wash the eels well, cut them in pieces as for stewing; season them with pepper and salt and a little beaten mace, according to your taste. Line the sides of your dish with crust, fill in the eels, and put as much water as the dish will hold, with a tablespoonful of catsup; put on the cover and bake it well.

162. *Directions for Cleansing Dried Currants and other Fruit.*—Put them into warm, not *hot* water: rub them thoroughly, take them out of the water into a sieve, leaving the sediment behind in the pan. Set the sieve in a pan of water, rub the currants well about in the sieve, changing the water till all the dirt is removed; let them drain, then dry them in a clean cloth and pick out all the refuse and stones, after which spread them on a large dish, and let them stand in the sun, or at a good distance from the fire, to dry and swell. Pack them in a jar for use.

Red and black currants should be held by the stalks, and dipped into a basin of water to remove the dust, then stripped into a dish. Cherries should be stalked and wiped, gooseberries should be picked and washed; strawberries, raspberries, etc., do not require to be washed, but merely to have the stalks taken off, raisins should be stoned and chopped; apples require to be cored and sliced.

163. *Cherry, Gooseberry, or Currant and Raspberry Pudding.*—Make a good crust, and line a pudding-basin, previously buttered, with it: pick your fruit and fill the basin; put in a very little water and some sugar, wet the edge of the paste all round, then cover the top with a crust and pinch the edges together; tie a cloth tightly over, and boil the pudding for an hour and a half, or two hours, according to its size. When you take it out of the pot dip the basin into cold water, then turn the pudding out on to a dish.

164. *Boiled Apple Pudding.*—Make a good paste, roll it out half an inch thick, but quite thin round the edge; pare and core apples sufficient to fill the crust· close it up, tie it up tight in a cloth, and boil it from two to three hours, according to the size. When it is done, turn it into a dish, cut a piece of crust out of the top, put in a good lump of butter, and as much sugar as will sweeten it to your taste, a little grated lemon-peel, and one drop of oil of cinnamon; stir it well in the pudding, lay on the crust, and send it to table hot.

165. *Rich Baked Apple Pudding.*—Pare twelve large apples, take out the cores, and put them into a saucepan with four or five spoonfuls of water; boil them till they are soft and thick; beat them well, and stir in a pound of loaf-sugar, the juice of three lemons, the peel of two lemons cut thin and beat fine in a mortar, two drops of oil of cinnamon, and the yolks of eight eggs beaten up; mix all together; put it in a puff paste, to bake it. When it is nearly done throw over it a little grated loaf-sugar.

166. *Apple Dumplings.*—Make a good paste, pare some large apples, cut them in quarters, take out the cores, and in place of them put in a clove and a piece of lemon-peel cut very thin; take a piece of crust enough for one apple, roll it round, put the quarters together, and roll the crust round it with a little flour in your hand. Have a pot of water boiling, take a clean cloth, dip it into the water, shake flour over it, and tie each dumpling by itself, put them in, and keep the water boiling all the time; if the apples be not large, half an hour will boil them. When they are done enough take them up, lay them on a dish, throw fine sugar over them, and send them to table with fresh melted butter in a boat and fine-beaten sugar in a saucer.

167. *Plain Suet Pudding.*—Chop a quarter of a pound of suet very fine, and mix it with half a pound of flour, a few bread-crumbs, and a little salt; when mixed together make it into a paste with a little water, not too stiff, dip your cloth into hot water, flour it, and tie up the pudding tight; put it into a saucepan of boiling water, and let it boil for an hour and a half. This is made richer by adding a couple of eggs, and using milk instead of water.

168. *Currant Dumplings.*—Pick and wash a pound of currants, dry them, and lay them on a plate before the fire. Chop a pound of suet very small, and put it into eight spoonfuls of flour, with two teaspoonfuls of salt, and three of ginger; now add the currants, and mix all well together; then beat up four eggs with a pint of milk; add this by degrees to the other ingredients, and make it into a light paste; roll it up into balls as large as a turkey's egg, with a little flour; flatten them a little and put them into boiling water; move them gently, that they may not stick together. Half an hour will boil them.

169. *Yorkshire Pudding.*—Mix up a quart of milk, four eggs, and a little salt, into a thick batter with flour, as for pancakes. Have a good piece of meat roasting at the fire; put a lump of dripping into a stewpan, and set it on the fire; when the fat boils pour in the pudding; let it bake till nearly done, then take away the dripping-pan and set the stewpan under the meat, that the gravy and dripping may drop on the pudding, and the heat of the fire may reach it and make it brown. When the meat is done, drain the fat from the pudding, slide it as dry as possible into a dish, and serve it up with the meat.

170. *Currant Bolster Pudding.*—Make a good paste, and roll it out very thin; have ready some currants well picked and washed, which strew pretty thickly all over the paste, roll it up, scald and flour your cloth, and roll the pudding in it; after which tie the cloth tightly at each end, put it into boiling water, and let it boil

for an hour and a half or two hours. Jelly, jam, or mincemeat is very good, spread over the paste, instead of currants.

171. *Plum Pudding.*—Take half a pound of flour, a pound of stale bread-crumbs, a pound of beef chopped fine, a pound of currants well picked, washed, and dried, a pound of raisins stoned and chopped, three-quarters of a pound of soft sugar, a quarter of a pound of candied orange and lemon peel, an ounce of powdered cinnamon, half an ounce of ground ginger, a nutmeg grated, twelve bitter almonds blanched and grated; and a little salt; mix these well together; then beat up seven eggs, strain them through a sieve, and add a little sweet milk if required. Stir this well into the other ingredients; make it thick, but not too stiff. Just before you are going to boil it stir into it a glass of rum or brandy, scald a cloth, flour it, and lay it in a basin; pour in your pudding; then have ready another cloth, also scalded and floured, which lay over the top, tie it round tightly, and put it in boiling water, of which there should be abundance, as well as plenty of room. Keep it boiling for six or seven hours. When it is done take it out of the pot, let it stand a few minutes to cool, or dip it into cold water; then turn it out into a dish, and serve it with caudle-sauce. A plain pudding may be made by using less fruit and spices.

172. *Bread Pudding.*—Crumble down stale bread in a dish; boil sufficient milk, which pour on the bread. Cover it up for a quarter of an hour, that the bread may swell; then beat it up to a fine pulp, stirring in a lump of butter. Now beat up three or four eggs, ground cinnamon, ginger, grated lemon-peel, and sugar to taste; half a pound of raisins stoned and chopped; half a pound of currants picked and washed; with a little salt. Mix this among the bread; make it of the consistence of thick batter. Butter the dish, pour it in, and bake it for half an hour.

173. *Bread and Butter Pudding.*—Cut some slices of thin bread and butter, and have ready some currants picked and washed. Butter a dish, and lay slices of the bread and butter on the bottom of it; then stew some currants over them, then lay another row of bread and butter, then some more currants, until the dish be full. Then beat up four eggs, add a pint of new milk, a little ground cinnamon, nutmeg, grated lemon-peel, four or five bitter almonds blanched and crushed, and sugar to your taste; also a very little salt. Mix all these together, and pour them over the bread and butter. Bake it half an hour.

174. *Hard Dumplings.*—Make a stiff paste of flour and water with a little salt. Boil them with salt beef or pickled pork.

175. *Custard Pudding.*—Beat up six eggs, add a quart of new milk, a little lemon-peel shred fine, five or six bitter almonds blanched and grated or crushed, with sugar to your taste; mix all together; then have ready your dish covered with a good puff-paste, into which pour the custard; grate over it half a nutmeg, and bake it; or put it into a basin without paste, tie a cloth over it, and boil it. If boiled, serve it with melted butter.

176. *Boiled Rice Pudding.*—Pick and wash your rice, put it into a clean saucepan with plenty of water, but without a cloth; let it boil till the grains are swelled and soft, which they will be in

about twenty minutes after it boils; then strain off the water, and set the saucepan on the hob, that the rice may be perfectly dry; put it into a buttered mould or basin to set; then turn it out, and pour sweet sauce over it.

177. *Baked Rice Pudding.*—Boil a quarter of a pound of rice in a quart of new milk, and stir it that it may not burn; when it begins to thicken take it off, let it stand till cool, then stir in a lump of butter, sugar to your palate, and some grated nutmeg; butter the dish, pour it in, and bake it. Raisins, currants, or sliced apples may be stirred in if liked.

178. *Rich Rice Pudding.*—Pick and wash a quarter of a pound of rice; put it on in cold water, and let it boil for five minutes, then strain the water off and put the rice on again in as much new milk as it will require to boil it quite soft, with a good pinch of salt; stir it frequently to prevent it burning; when done, put it in a large basin to cool. Beat up six eggs, a pint of milk, and sugar to your taste; it should be rather too sweet when you make it, as the sweetness goes off in the baking; add also five or six bitter almonds blanched and crushed, with plenty of lemon-peel chopped very fine; mix all well together, then stir it into the rice, taking care to mix it thoroughly, so that there be no lumps. Butter your dish, and pour in the mixture; and then shred about two ounces of beef suet as finely as possible all over the top; grate over that half a nutmeg, and bake it half an hour in a moderate oven.

179. *Tapioca Pudding.*—Take six tablespoonfuls of tapioca, and soak it in milk for some hours before you intend to use it; when you are going to make your pudding, put the tapioca into a quart of milk, place it on the fire, and, as soon as it boils, sweeten it to your taste, and let it simmer for a quarter of an hour; be very careful that it does not burn to the pot. Pour it into a basin, and stir into it a little fresh butter and three eggs beaten; butter your dish, pour it in, and bake it for an hour. If you wish it boiled, you must add another egg and boil it for an hour and a half. Sago-pudding may be made the same way.

180. *Yeast Dumplings.*—Make a light dough, as for bread, with flour, water, salt, and yeast; cover it with a cloth, and set it before the fire for half an hour; then have a saucepan of boiling water, make the dough into round balls, the size of a hen's egg, and put them in. Ten minutes will boil them; be sure to keep the water boiling all the time, or they will sink and be heavy. When they are done enough, which they will be in rather less than ten minutes, take them out with a slice, put them into a hot dish, and send up melted butter and sugar in a boat.

181. *Lemon Pudding.*—Take the yolks of six eggs well beaten, with a quarter of a pound of sugar; take a quarter of a pound of butter melted in as little water as possible; be careful not to oil it; keep stirring it till cold; then mix all together with the juice of two lemons, and the peel grated in. Cover your dish with a thin puff-paste, pour in the mixture, and bake it for half an hour.

182. *Snow-balls.*—Swell rice in milk; strain it, and lay it round some apples, previously pared and cored; put a bit of cinnamon, lemon-peel, and a clove in each, then tie them in a cloth and boil them well; they are eaten with melted butter and sugar.

183. *Batter Pudding.*—Beat up six eggs, take a quart of milk, six spoonfuls of flour, eight bitter almonds blanched and grated, a teaspoonful of salt, and one of ground ginger; mix all together, butter your basin, and pour it in; tie a cloth over it and boil it an hour and a quarter. When it is done, turn it into a dish and pour melted butter and sugar over it.

184. *Batter Pudding without Eggs.*—Use a quart of milk, mix six spoonfuls of flour with a little of the milk first, add the rest by degrees, with a teaspoonful of salt, two of beaten ginger, and two of the tincture of saffron; mix all together quite smooth, and boil it for an hour either in a buttered cloth or basin.

185. *Peas Pudding.*—Pick and well wash the best split peas, tie them loosely in a cloth, and let them boil for two or three hours, untie the cloth, and mash the peas with a wooden spoon till quite smooth; put in a good lump of butter, and pepper and salt, tie up the pudding again, and boil it for another half hour. It is then ready.

186. *Norfolk Dumplings.*—Take half a pint of milk, two eggs, and a little salt; make it into a batter with flour. Have ready a clean saucepan of boiling water, into which drop the batter. Let the water boil fast, and two or three minutes will boil them enough; then throw them into a sieve to drain the water from them, turn them into a dish, and stir a lump of butter among them. Eat them hot.

187. *Curate, or Sponge-Pudding.*—Beat up two eggs with their weight in flour, in good fresh butter and in pounded sugar; add two drops of essence of lemon; when well mixed pour it into four tea-cups, previously well buttered, and bake in a moderately quick oven. To be served with wine-sauce in a boat, not poured over the puddings. This dish is fit for any table; it is quickly and easily made, and if not eaten as pudding with sauce, is exceedingly good as cake when cold.

188. *Cabinet Pudding.*—Over six sponge-cakes pour sufficient sherry to soak them thoroughly; meanwhile beat up six new-laid eggs with a quart of new milk, sweetening with pounded loaf sugar. Put your cakes into the custard without beating them together, and turn the whole into a mould or basin, previously well buttered; tie a paper over the top, and steam the pudding for an hour. For sauce, beat up the yolks of eggs and sherry; heat them over the fire, not allowing them to boil, but keep whisking them all the time. Pour this over the pudding.

189. *Pancakes.*—Beat up three eggs and a quart of milk; make it up into a batter with flour, a little salt, a spoonful of ground ginger, and a little grated lemon-peel; let it be of a fine thickness and perfectly smooth. Clean your frying pan thoroughly, and put into it a good lump of dripping or butter; when it is hot pour in a cupful of batter, and let it run all over of an equal thickness; shake the pan frequently, that the batter may not stick, and when you think it is done on one side toss it over; if you cannot, turn it with a slice; and when both sides are of a nice light brown, lay it on a dish before the fire; strew sugar over it, and so do the rest. They should be eaten directly, or they will become heavy.

190. *Fruit Fritters.*—Make a batter of flour, milk, and eggs, of

whatever richness you desire; stir into it either raspberries, currants, or any other fruit. Fry in hot lard, the same as pancakes.

191. *Apple Fritters.*—Make batter as above, only thicker; pare apples; cut them in quarters, and core them; then take up a quarter of apple, with some batter, and fry then on both sides, in hot fat, the same as pancakes.

192. *Hasty Pudding.*—Boil a quart of milk with four bay-leaves; beat up the yolks of two eggs and a little salt; stir in the milk; then take out the bay-leaves, and with a wooden spoon in one hand with the other sprinkle in flour, and keep stirring it till it is of a good thickness. Let it boil, and keep it stirring; then pour it into the dish, and stick pieces of butter here and there.

PASTRY, CONFECTIONERY, BREAD, &c.

193. *Bread.*—Put a peck of good flour into a pan or trough, and mix with it three pints of warm water and half a pint of good yeast; stir it well with the hands till it becomes tough; leave it to rise; then add another two quarts of warm water and a quarter of a pound of salt; knead it well, and cover a cloth over it; then begin to heat the oven; by the time it is hot enough the dough will be ready to put in. Make up the dough into loaves of three pounds each; clean out the oven, and set in the bread; close the oven-door, and keep it shut till the bread is done, which will be in about two hours. Some persons mix boiled potatoes mashed with the flour; they make the bread lighter.

194. *French Bread and French Rolls.*—Mix the yolks of twelve eggs and the whites of eight, beaten and strained, a peck of fine flour, and a quart of good yeast (but not bitter), with as much warm milk as will make the whole into a thin, light dough; stir it well, but do not knead it. Put the dough into dishes, and set it to rise; then turn it into a quick oven; when done rasp the loaves.

French rolls are made by rubbing into every pound of flour an ounce of butter, one egg beaten, a little yeast, and sufficient milk to make a dough moderately stiff; beat it up, but do not knead it. Let it rise, and bake in rolls on tins; when baked, rasp them.

195. *Fine Rolls.*—Warm a bit of butter in half a pint of milk; add to it two spoonfuls of small-beer yeast and some salt; with these ingredients mix two pounds of flour; let it rise an hour, and knead it well; form the rolls, and bake them in a quick oven for twenty minutes.

196. *Tea Cakes.*—These are prepared the same as bread, substituting for the water warm milk, with a little butter melted in it, and sugar; let it rise; knead it into thin cakes, which bake on an iron plate over the fire.

197. *Yorkshire Cakes.*—Beat three pounds of flour, a pint and a half of warm milk, four spoonfuls of yeast, and four eggs, well together; then let them rise in the tins before you bake. Put them in a slow oven.

198. *To Make a Plum Cake.*—Take half a quartern of dough,

put it into a pan, and mix well into it half a pound of butter, half a pound of sugar, one pound of currants, a little mixed spice, a few carraway-seeds, some candied orange and lemon peel shred fine, a few bitter almonds blanched and crushed, and two eggs; knead these ingredients well together; butter your tin; pour in the cake and bake it.

199. *Pound Cake.*—Take of flour, butter, and powdered sugar, of each one pound, eight yolks and four whites of eggs, and a few carraway seeds; first beat up the butter to a cream—keep beating it one way—then gradually beat in the eggs, sugar, and flour. Bake it in a warm oven for an hour and a quarter. Cover the sides and bottom of the tin with buttered paper.

200. *Seed Cake.*—To half a quartern of dough put about six ounces of good dripping, the same quantity of sugar, a few carraway-seeds, and one egg. Mix all together, put it in a tin, or deep dish, and bake it.

201. *Ginger Nuts.*—Six pounds of flour, a pound and a quarter of butter rubbed into a pound and three-quarters of sugar; a quart of treacle, four ounces of ginger, a nutmeg, and a little cinnamon. Make the dough stiff, and then knead it hard for some time. Cut them into cakes, and bake. They will keep good a long while in a closely-covered stone jar.

202. *Gingerbread.*—Use three pounds of treacle, four beaten eggs, a pound of brown sugar, two ounces of finely powdered ginger; and of cloves, mace, and nutmeg, a quarter of an ounce each; of fine coriander and carraway-seeds, one ounce each; and four pounds of butter melted. Mix the whole together, and add as much flour as will knead it into a very stiff paste; roll it out, cut it into what form you choose, and bake it in a moderate oven.

203. *Arrowroot Blancmange.*—Take a quart of sweet milk, put about three parts of it into a saucepan, sweeten it with white sugar, and set it on the fire. Mix three tablespoonfuls of arrowroot with the rest of the milk, using a little at a time, so as to have it completely smooth and well-mixed. When the milk in the saucepan boils pour in the arrowroot, stirring it quickly, to prevent it being lumpy; it will thicken immediately. Let it boil for two or three minutes. Wet a mould with cold milk, and pour in the arrowroot, after stirring in two or three drops of oil of lemons. Let it stand till cold, then turn it out on a glass or china dish.

204. *Gooseberry Fool.*—Pick a quart of full-grown unripe gooseberries, and put them into a saucepan with a little water. Cover them up and let them simmer very softly. When they are tender, but not so much done as to burst, take them off, strain the water from them, and turn them into a dish. Now bruise them to a fine pulp, and sweeten them with sugar to your taste. Let them stand till cool, and then add new milk or cream.

205. *Gooseberry Jam.*—To every pound of red rough gooseberries add a pound of sugar; bruise the gooseberries in a mortar, and boil them well. When cold put the jam in pots.

206. *Blackberry Jam.*—Allow three-quarters of a pound of brown sugar to a pound of fruit. Boil the fruit half an hour; then add the sugar, and boil all together for ten minutes.

207. Raspberry Jam.—Allow a pound of sugar to each pound of fruit; press them with a spoon in an earthen dish, add the sugar, and boil all together for fifteen minutes.

208. Strawberry Jam is made in the same way.

209. Calf's-Foot Jelly.—Boil two calf's-feet in half a gallon of water till it is reduced to a quart; strain it, let it stand till cold, skim off the fat, and take the jelly up clean; whatever sediment remains at the bottom, leave it. Put the jelly into a saucepan with a pint of mountain wine, half a pound of loaf sugar, and the juice of four lemons; then beat up six whites of eggs with a whisk, put them into a saucepan, and stir all together till it boils. When it has boiled a few minutes have ready a large flannel-bag and pour it in. It will run through quickly, therefore pour it in repeatedly till it runs clear; then have ready a large basin, with the lemon-peels cut into it as thin as possible; let the jelly run into it, and the peels will impart to it both a rich amber color and a fine flavor. Fill the glasses with a clean silver spoon.

210. Red Currant Jelly.—Pick the currants from the stalks and put them into stone jars; set them in a cool oven till they are soft; then strain them off, and to every pint of juice add one pound of loaf sugar pounded. Boil the syrup about twenty minutes, skimming it all the time; pour it into the pots boiling hot, as it will set the sooner. Lay brandied paper on the top.

211. Black Currant Jelly may be made in the same way; only common brown sugar may be used.

212. Apple Jelly.—Take two dozen of large golden pippins or golden russets, pare them, and put in as much water as will cover them; let them boil as fast as possible till the apples are reduced to a pulp; strain them through a jelly-bag, and to every pint of jelly put one pound of fine sugar; boil it over a quick fire for a quarter of an hour, add lemon-juice to your taste, keep it boiling, and skim it. Try a little on a plate; when it jellies, or sets, it is boiled enough.

213. Rhubarb Jam.—Peel the stalks, and cut them up about an inch long; put them into a broad tin or copper pan with sufficient water to let them float. Let it boil till reduced to a pulp, keeping it well stirred from the bottom. Pass the pulp through a colander or coarse sieve, and to each pint add from three-quarters of a pound to a pound of sugar, either loaf or moist; put it back into the pan and boil it for another half hour, still keeping it stirred. Try now, by dropping a little on a plate, if it is done enough; it should be of the consistence of jelly; if it spread, boil it a little longer, till stiff beneath the finger. Pour it into pots or jars, and when cold, cover and tie it down like other preserves.

214. Orange Marmalade.—Cut and squeeze Seville oranges according to the quantity you desire to make; then take out the pulp, leaving the rind very thin, which shred quite fine, and boil till tender. Then boil the pulp quite soft and rub it through a hair-sieve; now mix the juice, pulp, and chips together, and to every pound add one pint of clarified sugar. Boil the sugar till it snaps, then add the other ingredients. Let them boil ten minutes and put them into pots.

HOME-MADE WINES AND COOLING BEVERAGES.

215. *Gooseberry.*—Gather when half ripe, in dry weather. Pick clean, put a peck into a vessel; bruise with a piece of wood, being careful to keep the seeds whole. Put the pulp into a canvas bag, press out the juice; to 1 gallon of which add about 2 pounds of fine loaf sugar; mix the whole by stirring with a stick, and when the sugar is dissolved, pour into a cask which will exactly contain it. If the quantity be 9 gallons, stand for a fortnight; if 20, 40 days; and so in proportion, taking care to keep it cool. After standing the proper time, draw off from the lees, and put into another clean vessel of equal size, or the same, after pouring away the lees, and making it clean. Let a cask of ten or twelve gallons stand about three months, and 20 gallons 5 months, after which bottle it off.

216. *Elder.*—Pick berries when ripe, put into a stone jar, set them in a kettle of boiling water or an oven till the jar is hot through, then take them out, strain through a coarse sieve; squeeze the berries, and put the juice into a clean vessel. To 1 quart of juice put one pound of sugar; boil, and skim clean. When clear, pour into a cask. Close up, let it stand 6 months, then bottle, fining it by adding to every 10 gallons 1 oz. of isinglass dissolved in cider, a quart of brandy and 6 eggs.

217. *Ginger.*—To 7 gallons of water put 19 pounds of sugar, boil for half an hour, removing scum as it rises; then take a small quantity of the liquor, add it to 9 ozs. of the best ginger bruised. Put all together, when nearly cold, chop 9 pounds of raisins very small, and put them into a 9 gallon cask. Slice 4 lemons into the cask after taking seeds, pour the liquor over them, with half a pint of fresh yeast. Leave it unstopped for 3 weeks, keeping it filled up, and in 6 or 9 months will be fit for bottling.

218. *Red Currant.*—Gather currants in dry weather; put into a pan and bruise with a wooden pestle; let them stand about 20 hours, after which strain through a sieve; add 3 pounds of finely powdered sugar to every gallon of the liquor, and, after shaking well, fill the vessel. If it does not prove clear in 2 or 3 months, draw off into another vessel, and let it stand a few days previous to bottling.

219. *Raspberry.*—Gather them ripe; husk and bruise; strain through a bag into jars or other vessels. To 1 gallon of juice allow 1 1-2 lb. of loaf sugar. When dissolved, decant liquor into a cask. When fermented, add 1 pint of white wine, or 1-2 a pint of proof spirits to every gallon contained in the cask, and hang a bag in it containing 1 oz. of bruised mace. In three months, if kept cool, will be fit for use.

220. *Mulberry.*—Gather on a dry day, when just changed from redness to a shining black; spread thinly on a fine cloth, or a clean floor or table, 24 hours, then press them. Boil 1 gallon of water for 1 gallon of juice, putting 1 oz. of cinnamon-bark, and 6 ozs. of sugar-candy finely powdered, to each gallon of water. When the water is taken off and settled, skim and strain, and put it to the mulberry-juice. Add to 1 gallon of the mixture a pint of white or Rhenish wine. Let stand in a cask to ferment for 5 or 6 days. When settled, draw off into bottles. Keep cool.

221. *Damson.*—Take a good quantity of damsons and common plums, which should be tolerably ripe, slit in halves, so that the stones will come out, then wash gently, and add a little water and honey. To every gallon of the pulp, put a gallon of spring water, with a few cloves and bay-leaves; boil the mixture, and add as much sugar as will well sweeten it; skim off froth, and let it cool. Now press the fruit, squeezing out the liquor; strain through a fine strainer, and put the water and juice together into a cask. Let it stand and ferment for 3 or 4 days: fine with whites of eggs; draw off into bottles and cork well. In 12 days it will be ripe.

222. *Raisin.*—Wash well, pick them from the stalks: to 1 pound thus prepared and chopped, add 1 quart of water which has been boiled and become cold; add to every 10 gallons 6 pounds of fine sugar. Let the whole stand for a month, stirring it frequently. Then take the raisins from the cask, and stop the liquor closely in the vessel. In the course of a month, let it be racked into another vessel, leaving all the sediment behind. This must be repeated till it becomes fine; then add 1 dozen Seville oranges, the rinds being pared very thin, and infused in 2 quarts of brandy, which add to the liquor at its last racking. Let it stand in the cask 3 months, when it will be fit for bottling. Should remain in bottle 12 months.

223. *Grape.*—Put 1 gallon of soft water to 1 gallon of ripe grapes, bruise and let stand a week, stirring occasionally; then draw the liquor off fine. To one gallon of wine put two pounds of loaf sugar; put into a vessel, but do not stop it till it has done hissing; then stop close, and in 6 months will be fit to bottle.

224. *Orange.*—Take 200 oranges, peel very thin, put peels into 18 gallons of water, let them boil for 10 or 12 hours, till color and taste are all extracted. Squeeze into it the juice of the oranges through a sieve, add 1-2 cwt. of sugar, and stir till all is dissolved. Let it stand for 3 or 4 days, then barrel it, and put in 6 pounds of raisins and a gallon of brandy. Work it with a little yeast on toast, keep the cask filled, and when done working, bung up for 12 months; then bottle off, and it will keep for twenty years.

225. *Effervescing Draught.*—Beat in a mortar 1 oz. tartaric acid; divide into 24 parts, put each part into a *blue* paper; pound 1 oz. of bi-carbonic of soda, dividing into 24 parts, putting each part into *white* paper. These are then ready for use. When a draught is required, put the soda into a tumbler 1-2 filled with water; when dissolved, add acid. Drink while effervescing.

226. *Effervescing Fruit Drinks.*—Put strawberries, raspberries, or blackberries into good vinegar, then strain it off, adding fresh fruit till the flavor is sufficiently strong. Bottle, and when about to use, dissolve a very small teaspoonful of soda in a little water; when the lumps are melted, fill up the tumbler two-thirds, add the fruit-vinegar. Should be drank immediately after it is mixed.

227. *Ginger Beer.*—Put into 6 quarts of water 1 large spoonful of ginger, 1 also of cream of tarter, 1 pint of treacle, and 1-4 of a pint of home-brewed yeast. When it begins to ferment, bottle it.

228. *Lemonade.*—Shave the rind of 2 lemons very thin into a jug, remove the pith, and cut the fruit in thin slices on the peel; add 1-4 lb. of loaf sugar, and pour over all a quart of boiling water. An agreeable beverage either hot or cold.

HOW

TO

PICKLE

AND

PRESERVE.

HOW TO PICKLE.

THE strongest and best vinegar should be used for pickling. It must not be boiled, or the strength of the vinegar and spices will be evaporated. By parboiling the pickles in brine, they will be ready in much less time than they are when done in the usual manner of soaking them in cold salt and water for six or eight days. When taken out of the hot brine, let them get cold and quite dry before you put them into the pickle.

To assist the preservation of pickles a portion of salt is added, and for the same purpose, and to give flavor, long pepper, black pepper, allspice, ginger, cloves, mace, garlic, eschalots, mustard, horseradish, and capsicum.

The following is the best method of preparing the pickle; it is as cheap as any, requires less care than any other way:—Bruise in a mortar four ounces of the above spices, put them into a stone jar with a quart of the strongest vinegar, stop the jar closely with a bung, cover that with a bladder soaked with pickle, and set it on a trivet by the side of the fire for three days, well shaking it up three or four times in the day. The jar being well closed, and the infusion being made with a mild heat, there is no loss by evaporation.

To enable the articles pickled more easily and speedily to imbibe the flavor of the pickle they are immersed in, previously to pouring it on them, run a larding pin through them in several places, or prick them with a fork.

Pickles should be kept in a dry place, in unglazed earthenware, or glass jars, which are preferable, as you can, without opening them, observe whether they want filling up; they must be very carefully stopped with well-fitted bungs, and tied over as closely as possible with a bladder wetted with the pickle.

When the pickles are all used, boil up the liquor with a little fresh spice.

To walnut liquor may be added a few anchovies and eschalots; let it stand till it is quite clear, and bottle it; thus you may furnish your table with an excellent savory keeping sauce for hashes, made dishes, fish, &c., at very small cost.

Jars should not be more than three parts filled with the articles pickled, which should be covered with pickle at least two inches above their surface; the liquor wastes, and all of the articles pickled that are not covered are soon spoiled.

When they have been done about a week open the jars and fill them up with pickle. If you discern in them any symptoms of not keeping well do them over again in fresh vinegar and spice.

Tie a wooden spoon, full of holes, or a wooden fork, round each jar, to take them out with; and if you take out more pickles than you require to use, do not put what is left back into the jar.

If you wish to have your pickles of a nice, but perfectly harmless green, nothing succeeds better than boiling the vegetables in water made slightly alkaline, sometimes either with a small quantity of bicarbonate of of soda, sometimes with lime-water, and sometimes with saccharate of lime, or with water containing a quarter of an ounce of liquid ammonia to the quart.

If you wish cauliflowers, onions, etc., to be white, use distilled vinegar for them.

Last of all, do not use brass or copper kettles for pickling; as the verdigris produced in them by the vinegar is of a most poisonous nature when the vinegar is allowed to cool in them. Glazed kettles are the best, but if you cannot procure them, block tin may be substituted. Iron is apt to discolor any acid that is boiled in it.

RED CABBAGE.

Red cabbage should be pickled in September. Having taken off the large outside leaves, cut the cabbage into quarters, taking out the stalk. Then shred the whole into a colander, and sprinkle with salt, in which let them remain for about twenty-four hours, when they must be drained and put into a jar, and have the following pickle poured over them cold: To each quart of vinegar put an ounce of ground black pepper, half an ounce of pounded ginger, some salt, and horseradish cut in slices, and a few capsicums or cayenne, according to taste. Put all these into a jar stopped close, and let them steep three days on a trivet by the side of the fire, and when cold strain the liquor through a cloth, and pour it on the cabbage.

ONIONS.

Choose small button onions, as near of a size as possible; throw them into warm water, which will prevent their affecting the eyes so much while peeling them. As they are peeled, throw them into a strong brine of salt and water; let them remain in this till the next day; then put them on the fire, and boil them in it for a minute. Or, as they are peeled, throw them into milk and water. Drain them from this when they are all done; put them into a jar, and pour the brine on them boiling hot. Cover them close, and set them aside till the next day. Drain, and dry them in a cloth; put them into cold distilled vinegar, with a few blades of bruised ginger, some whole pepper, and, if approved, a little mace and sliced horseradish. Keep them always well covered with vinegar. Cork the jar close, and put it in a cool, dry place.

FRENCH BEANS OR GHERKINS.

Put the beans or gherkins into a brine of salt and water made strong enough to float an egg; let them remain in this for four or five days, or a week; take them from the brine, and put them into a saucepan with equal quantities of vinegar and water sufficient for them to float in; heat them in this until it is scalding hot or almost boiling, but it must not boil. Keep them at this heat

HOW TO PICKLE AND PRESERVE.

for an hour or two, and put them into a jar or pan to cool, in the liquor they were scalded in. If they are not sufficiently green, heat them again, and let them cool as before. That is the proper way to preserve the green color. When cold, drain the vinegar and water from them, and put them into cold vinegar with bruised ginger, whole allspice, mace, and pepper. Cork the jars close, tie them over with leather or pieces of bladder, and keep them in a cool, dry place.

Gherkins for pickling should be about the size of a finger, smaller than this they have not attained their flavor; French beans, quite young, or before they are half grown.

CUCUMBERS.

Cucumbers may be preserved in the same manner as the French beans and gherkins, or the skin may be thinly pared off, and each cut in two, the seeds taken out, and preserved like the preceding, or as follows:—Cut a piece from the end of each, leaving it hanging to a bit of the skin, scoop out the seeds, and put them into a strong brine. Take them out at the expiration of a week; fill the insides with equal parts of mustard-seed, ground ginger, and pepper, mixed with some small onions peeled, or a few heads of garlic and some whole allspice. Sew or tie on the top again, green, and finish them as gherkins.

Melons and mangoes are prepared in the same way.

Cucumbers for pickling should be full grown, but not overgrown; melons, half grown.

CAULIFLOWERS OR BROCOLI.

The whitest and firmest cauliflowers that can be obtained should be chosen for this purpose. Cut or break the flowers into small branches, and put them into salt and water for a week or ten days. The brine, or pickle, should be made strong enough with salt for an egg to float on the surface. Take them from the brine, and put them into a saucepan of clean water. Let them boil for about ten minutes or a quarter of an hour, or until they begin to get tender; but they must not be done, or they will lose their crispness. Drain them from the water, and spread them on a coarse cloth, or on sieves, and put them to dry in the sun until all the moisture is evaporated; then put them into a jar, and cover them with distilled or white wine vinegar. Mace, long pepper, white peppercorns, and a few grains of allspice, may be added to the vinegar, which should be kept warm for some time by the side of the fire to extract the flavor of the spice, but must not be allowed to boil. Pour the vinegar over the cauliflower when it is cold. Cork the jar close, and put it aside for use. Fill the jar occasionally with vinegar, as the flowers absorb it.

WALNUTS.

Take large, full-grown walnuts, but they must be tender, so that they can be easily pierced with a needle. Lay them in salt and water for two days, then shift them into another weak brine; in a couple of days put them into fresh water for two days longer, after which take them out and lay them on a board, so that they may not touch each other; let them stay in the sun for a day or two till they are perfectly dry, and turn black. Then put them into a clean, dry stone jar, and for every hundred walnuts allow half a pint of mustard-seed, half an ounce of black pepper, half an ounce of allspice, a quarter of an ounce of mace, six bay-leaves, and a stick of horseradish sliced; mix these ingredients with the walnuts, which should fill the jar, and fill up with boiling vinegar. Put a plate on the top, and, when cold, tie them down closely with bladder and leather. They will be ready for use in two or three months; meanwhile they must be examined occasionally, and kept covered with vinegar. Some persons put in an onion stuck with cloves, and some sliced ginger.

Another Way.—Take a hundred walnuts, wipe them, prick them with a large needle, and put them into a jar, sprinkling, as you lay them in, the following spices mixed: Cloves, allspice, nutmeg, whole pepper, and sliced ginger, of each an ounce; half a pint of mustard-seed, four cloves of garlic, and a stick of horseradish; then add two tablespoonfuls of salt, and sufficient boiling vinegar to cover the whole. Cover the jar as above, and when cold tie down closely.

The liquor makes excellent catsup for flavoring steaks, chops, sauces, and stews.

Another Way.—Put green walnut shells into a brine of salt and water strong enough to float an egg; let them lie covered in this ten or twelve days; take them out, and lay them in the sun for a week; put them into a jar, and pour boiling vinegar on them; in about a week or ten days pour off the vinegar, make it boiling hot, and pour over them again. In a month it will be fit for use, and will be found excellent to eat with cold meat, and particularly useful in making many sauces.

CELERY.

Separate the stalks from the heads; cleanse them thoroughly, and put them into salt and water strong enough to bear an egg. Let them remain in this for a week or ten days, or until wanted to pickle; then take them out, wash them well in clean water, drain dry, place in a jar and pour boiling vinegar over, to which any approved spices may have been added, as is usual for pickling. Keep it well covered with vinegar. If the celery be allowed to remain a long time in salt and water, it will be necessary to soak it in clean water for a day or two, changing the water occasionally.

BEETROOT.

Beetroots should be pickled in September. To pickle beetroots, boil them till three-parts done; then, when cold, peel them and cut them into thin slices; put the cut slices into a jar, and pour on them hot spiced vinegar, sufficient to cover the whole. After they have stood a month they will be fit for use, and will be found an excellent and wholesome pickle.

NASTURTIUMS.

There are two varieties of nasturtium—the major and minor; both yield seeds fit for pickling, which are an excellent substitute for capers. The young shoots are equally as good as the seeds for pickling, and their flavor improves an ordinary salad when not used in excess. The method of pickling nasturtium is as follows: Fill any jar with the nasturtium seeds or shoots, then pour on them boiling vinegar, to which add a good seasoning of salt. Boil up the vinegar every three days till the pickle is of a good color; then add a little ginger and whole pepper. Another way is to cover the seeds or shoots with strong brine, set the jar on the trivet, and keep them hot for three days; then pour off the brine, and pour on scalding vinegar, and keep them hot for a week or ten days till they are of good color; then add spice, such as ginger and pepper: or, better still, pour off the last vinegar, and add in its place spiced vinegar. The nasturtiums should be full grown, but not old; they are ready for pickling in September.

RED CAPSICUMS.

Red capsicums are pickled by simply putting them into cold vinegar, with a little whole allspice and mace. Lay green capsicums for three days in strong brine; drain them from this, and put them into cold distilled vinegar, with a little mace and whole allspice. Nasturtium-buds may also be done as these.

TOMATOES.

Peel them without putting them into water as before directed, slice them into a jar, add pepper and salt, and cover them with a good vinegar. Excellent with cold meat, or as a salad with a little oil.

Another Way.—Take any quantity of green tomatoes, and peel them. To two quarts of tomatoes add three or four small green capsicums, one pint of small onions, scalded in salt and water and peeled, half a pound of salt, and one pint of mustard-seed. Chop the whole fine, so as to make a mince. Strew over the bottom of a jar about two inches thick with the mince, then salt and mustard-seed, and again mince, until the whole is disposed of; set it away for a few days for the salt to dissolve, and cover with the best vinegar.

RADISH-PODS.

Boil some vinegar with salt and spice, and when cold put in the radish-pods; or they may be put into old vinegar, from which green pickles or onions have been taken—only boil it up afresh. Radish-pods make an excellent pickle, and, like nasturtiums, serve as a good substitute for capers.

CHEAP AND WHOLESOME PICKLES.

Take a jar with a close lid or bung, and half fill it with the best vinegar; then, as spare vegetables of any description come to hand, such as small beans, cauliflowers, radish-pods, young cucumbers, onions, &c., throw them in, taking care, as the jar fills, that there is sufficient vinegar to cover the vegetables. When nearly full, add mustard-seeds, bruised ginger, eschalots, whole pepper, &c., to taste. Tie down tightly and place the jar in a vessel of water over the fire, or in a slow oven until the articles are sufficiently soft to suit the palate. In this manner good, wholesome pickles can be made at only the expense of the vinegar and spice, and with the least possible amount of trouble. Of course, if the various kinds of vegetables are wished to be kept distinct, such may be done.

AMERICAN PICKLE.

To eight quarts of cold spring water add seven pounds of salt, ten ounces of saltpetre, and one pound of treacle; mix well together, and let it stand till the next day; it will then be ready to receive pork, beef, or tongues. This pickle possesses many advantages; the principal one is, that meat preserved in it never gets hard, or too salt; it will keep good from three to five months, according to the quantity of provisions cured in it.

PICCALILLI.

This is a mixture of all kinds of pickles. Select from the salt brine, of a uniform size and of various colors, small cucumbers, button onions, small bunches of cauliflowers, carrots cut in fanciful shape, turnips sliced, radishes, radish-pots, French beans, cayenne-pods, mace, ginger, long spice, strips of horseradish, &c. Arrange your selection tastefully in glass jars, and pour over them a liquor prepared in the following manner:—To one gallon of white wine vinegar add eight tablespoonfuls of salt, eight of mustard-flour, four of ground ginger, two of pepper, two of allspice, two of turmeric, and boil all together one minute; the mustard and turmeric must be mixed together with vinegar before they are put into the liquor; when the liquor has boiled pour it into a pan, cover it closely, and when it is cold pour it into the jars containing the pickles; cover the jars with cork, tie them down with bladder, and let them stand six months, when they will contain good pickles. Piccalilli is an excellent accompaniment to many highly seasoned dishes; if well put up, it will keep for years. If you like oil in the piccalilli, it should be well incorporated with the vinegar, and added with the other ingredients to the boiling liquor.

MIXED PICKLE AND INDIA PICKLE.

Fill a large jar half full of brine made strong enough to float an egg. Into this put, as convenient, various sort of vegetables that are usually pickled, such as small onions, radish-pods, scalded branches of cauliflowers, French beans, gherkins, and cucumbers sliced, also rock samphire, white cabbage sliced, celery, &c. These may lie in the salt and water until the whole is collected, without being injured, observing that the last article should be allowed to remain in the brine for ten or twelve days; then take them out and lay them on sieves, or spread out on cloths to drain and dry. When dry, pack them in a jar; cover them with cold vinegar, and let them remain for ten days or a fortnight (a month or two will make no difference), observing, if mixed pickle be required, to pour off the vinegar, boil it up, and pour over the pickles twice or three times; but for INDIA PICKLE, prepare a gallon of vinegar, more or less according to the quantity of pickles to be done, in the following manner:—Mix gradually a quarter of a pound of the best flour of mustard, and two ounces of powdered turmeric, with some of the cold vinegar at first, to ensure its being properly mixed; then add the rest, with a quarter of a pound of white mustard-seed. Bruise a quarter of a pound of ginger, two ounces of white pepper, and one ounce of chilies, and tie them in a muslin bag. Boil the whole gently for twenty minutes or half an hour, and pour it, whilst boiling, on the pickles, having previously drained off the vinegar they were first put in. In ten or twelve days repeat the boiling, pour it over the pickles whilst boiling hot, and they will be ready for use when cold.

HOW TO PRESERVE.

GENERAL RULES AND DIRECTIONS.

LET everything used for the purpose of preserving be perfectly clean and dry; bottles especially so.

Never place a preserving-pan flat upon the fire, as this will render the preserve liable to burn; but let it rest on a trivet, or on the lowered bar of the kitchen range.

After having added the sugar, stir the preserves gently, gradually increasing the motion, not ceasing until they are done; this precaution will always prevent the chance of their being spoiled.

Clear the scum off the top of the jam with a spoon as it rises.

Fruit which is to be preserved in syrup must first be blanched or boiled gently, until it becomes soft enough to absorb the sugar; and a thin syrup must be poured on it at first, or it will shrivel instead of remaining plump and becoming clear. Thus, if its weight of sugar is to be allowed, and boiled to a syrup with a pint of water to the pound, only half the weight must be taken at first, and this must not be boiled with the water more than fifteen or twenty minutes at the commencement of the process; a part of the remaining sugar must be added every time the syrup is reboiled, unless it should be otherwise directed in the receipt.

To preserve both the true flavor and the color of fruit in jams and jellies, boil them rapidly until they are well reduced, *before* the sugar is added, and quickly afterwards; but do not allow them to become so much thickened that the sugar will not dissolve in them easily and throw up its scum. In some seasons the juice is so much richer than in others, that this effect takes place almost before one is aware of it; but the drop which adheres to the skimmer, when it is held up, will show the state it has reached.

Never use tin, iron, or pewter spoons or skimmers for preserves, as they will convert the color of red fruit into a dingy purple, and impart, besides, a very unpleasant flavor.

When cheap jams or jellies are required, make them at once with loaf sugar, but use that which is *well refined* always, for preserves in general; it is a false economy to purchase an inferior kind, as there is great waste from it in the quantity of scum which it throws up.

Pans of copper or bell-metal are the proper utensils for preserving fruit: when used, they must be scoured bright with sand. Tinned pans turn and destroy the color of the fruit that is put into them. Stew-pans are also made of iron, glazed inside, which is very nice for preserving.

In clarifying sugar take the finest kind, break it into large lumps, and put it into a preserving-pan. If for syrup, add a pint of cold water to each pound; if for candying, a couple of wine-glassfuls to the pound will be sufficient. Beat the white of an egg, add it to the water, mix it well, and pour it over the sugar; one egg is enough for twelve pounds of sugar if it is fine, or two if it is coarse. When the sugar is nearly melted, stir it well, and put it over a gentle fire; do not stir it after the scum begins to rise; let it boil five minutes, then take it off the fire, let it stand a minute or two, then take the scum carefully off; put the pan again on the fire, and when the syrup begins to boil throw in a little cold water, which should be kept back for the purpose; boil till the scum rises, draw it off from the fire, and skim it as before; repeat this till quite clear; it is then fit for use. It is by long boiling that the differ ent degrees are acquired, which the confectioner requires.

A simple method of candying fruit is to lay some fruits from syrup into a clean sieve; to dip it quickly into hot water, and then put the fruit into a fine cloth to drain; sift over it refined sugar, and dry on sieves in a moderate oven.

A little powdered alum dissolved in water, and put into the syrup of preserves, with a full quantity of sugar, will sometimes prevent their candying.

The only secret of storing preserves is to exclude the air from them, and to set them in a dry place, not placing the pots on each other.

If preserves seem slightly damp, and unlikely to keep well, to save the waste of second boiling, remove the papers, and put the jars in a cool oven (after a batch of bread is drawn is as good a time as any), and let them remain until the preserves get thoroughly heated. When cold, cover them as before. Writing-paper, saturated with good olive oil, is better than steeping it in brandy to cover the tops of the preserves. Tie pieces of bladder or paper over this.

Fruit jellies may be preserved from mouldiness by covering the surface one-fourth of an inch deep with finely pulverized loaf sugar. Thus protected, they will keep in good condition for years.

All fruits for preserving should be gathered in dry weather; but, as this is not always practicable, much inconvenience may be obviated by boiling the fruits for jellies and jams long before the sugar is added. By so doing, the watery particles will evaporate, and the preserve will be better flavored by the sugar not being too long on the fire.

JAMS AND PRESERVES.

RASPBERRY JAM.

Take equal weights of fruit and moist sugar: put them on the fire together; keep stirring and breaking the fruit till the sugar melts, then boil till it will jelly on a plate.

Though simple, this will be found a very good receipt.

HOW TO PICKLE AND PRESERVE.

Another Way.—Take equal weights of fruit and roughly-pounded loaf sugar; bruise the fruit with the back of a spoon, and boil them together for half an hour; if a little more juice is wanted, add the juice of currants drawn as for jelly.

STRAWBERRY JAM.

Allow equal weights of pounded loaf sugar and of strawberries; mash them in the preserving-pan, and mix the sugar well with it; stir, scum, and boil it for twenty minutes.

BLACK CURRANT JAM.

Allow equal weights of clipped currants and of pounded loaf sugar; bruise and mash the fruit in a preserving-pan over the fire; add the sugar; stir it frequently; when it boils, skim, and let it boil for ten minutes.

WHITE OR RED CURRANT JAM.

Pick the fruit very nicely, and allow an equal quantity of finely-pounded loaf sugar; put a layer of each alternately into a preserving-pan, and boil for ten minutes; or they may be boiled the same length of time in sugar previously clarified and boiled candy high.

GRAPE JAM.

The grapes ought not to be very ripe. They should be carefully picked, and all that are at all injured should be rejected. To one pound of grapes add a half pound of sugar; no water but what hangs about them after they have been washed. Put the grapes into a cooking-pan, then a layer of sugar, then a layer of grapes. Boil on a moderate fire, stirring it all the time, to prevent its burning.

CHERRY JAM.

Stone four pounds of cherries, and put them in a preserving-pan with two pounds of fine white sugar and a pint of red currant juice. Boil the whole together rather fast, until it stiffens, and then put it into pots for use.

GOOSEBERRY JAM.

Stalk and crop six pounds of the *small, red, rough gooseberry*, put them into a preserving-pan, and, as they warm, stir and bruise them to bring out the juice. Let them boil for ten minutes, then add four pounds of sugar, and place it on the fire again; let it boil, and continue boiling for two hours longer, stirring it all the time to prevent its burning. When it thickens, and will jelly upon a plate, it is done enough. Put it into pots, and allow it to remain a day before it is covered.

BLACKBERRY JAM.

In families where there are many children there is no preparation of fruit so wholesome, so cheap, and so much admired, as this homely conserve. The fruit should be clean picked in dry weather, and to every pound of berries put a half pound of coarse brown sugar; boil the whole together for three-quarters of an hour or an hour, stirring it well the whole time. Put it in pots like any other preserve, and it will be found most useful in families; it is medicinal for children.

PINE-APPLE JAM.

Pare and weigh the pine-apples, and grate them down on a large grater. To one pound of fruit put three-quarters of a pound of powdered sugar; put it over the fire, and when it comes to a boil stir till done. Boil it half an hour or more till clear; put it in jars, and cover it carefully.

PINE-APPLES.

Take off the top and bottom of the pine, and pare the outside; put a pint of water, two pounds of loaf-sugar, one lemon (cut in slices), and the peeling of the pine, together, into a well-tinned saucepan; then boil them for about five minutes. Now strain the syrup, then cut up the pine-apple into thin slices, and put them with the strained syrup into the saucepan. The pine is now to be boiled till it is easily pricked with a sharp wooden skewer. The preserve is then fit for keeping in jars "as long as one can." The number of pines to a pint of syrup depends, of course, on their size.

RHUBARB.

Cut the rhubarb as for tarts, and to every quart give one pound of good moist sugar. Put the sugar over the rhubarb, and leave it twenty-four hours to draw out the juice. The sugar sinks, but is not dissolved. Boil the juice and sugar together for twenty minutes after it begins to boil just at the edge of the pan; then add the rhubarb, and boil slowly twenty minutes longer. There is no need to stir the syrup or preserve, if slowly boiled. The rhubarb and sugar do not require a warm place to draw out the juice. By this method the pieces of rhubarb remain separate from each other when the preserve is done. It keeps good a year, if kept in jars well dried, and in a dry place.

Or, procure six oranges, peel them, and take away the white rind and the kernels; then slice the pulp into the stewpan, along with the peel cut very small; add thereto one quart of rhubarb cut fine, and from one pound to one pound and a half of loaf sugar. Boil the whole down in the usual way, as for other preserves. Made in this manner it will be found almost equal to Scotch marmalade.

STRAWBERRIES OR RASPBERRIES, FOR CREAMS OR ICES, WITHOUT BOILING.

Let the fruit be gathered in the middle of a warm day, in very dry weather; strip it from the stalks directly, weigh it, turn it into a bowl or deep pan, and bruise it gently; mix with an equal weight of fine, dry, sifted sugar, and put it immediately into small, wide-necked bottles; cork these firmly without delay, and tie a bladder over the tops. Keep them in a cool place, or the fruit will ferment. The mixture should be stirred softly, and only just sufficiently to blend the sugar and the fruit. The bottles must be perfectly dry, and the bladders, after having been cleaned in the usual way, and allowed to become nearly so, should be moistened with a little spirit on the side which is to be next to the cork.

STRAWBERRIES.

To two pounds of fine large strawberries add two pounds of powdered sugar, and put them in a preserving-kettle, over a slow fire, till the sugar is melted: then boil them precisely twenty minutes, as fast as possible; have ready a number of *small* jars, and put the fruit in boiling hot. Cork and seal the jars immediately, and keep them through the summer in a cold, dry cellar. The jars must be heated before the hot fruit is poured in, otherwise they will break.

RASPBERRIES, WHOLE.

Take five quarts of raspberries, and cull from them about three pints of the largest and firmest, and set them aside; put the remainder in the preserving pan, and put them on the fire to extract the juice. When they are boiled enough let them cool, and then strain them through a cloth. While they are cooling boil up the sugar in the proportion of one pound to one quart of the fruit; and when you have removed the scum, and it is a good syrup, throw in your whole raspberries; let them boil rapidly a few minutes, but be careful they do not fall to pieces or become ragged. Take them out with a skimmer full of holes, and spread them over a large dish to cool; then throw into the syrup the juice of those you have previously boiled, and let it boil till it is nearly a jelly; throw in again the whole fruit, and give it a smart boil; then put it in your jars hot, and do not cover them till cold.

DAMSONS.

To every pound of damsons allow three-quarters of a pound of powdered sugar; put into jars of well-glazed earthen pots, alternately a layer of damsons and one of sugar; tie strong paper or cloth over the pots, and set them in the oven after the bread is drawn, and let them stand till the oven is cold. The next day strain off the syrup, and boil it till thick; when it is cold, put the damsons into small jars or glasses, pour over the syrup, which should cover them, and tie a wet bladder or strong cloth over them.

GREENGAGES IN SYRUP.

Those should be chosen which are not quite ripe. Let them be sound, and as fresh-gathered as possible. Prick them several times to the stone with a fork or needle, and throw them into a pan of cold water as they are done. Put them into a preserving-pan, and let them heat gradually until the water is scalding hot; keep them at this heat for an hour or two; then take them off, and cover them with vine or cabbage leaves, and let them get cold in the water they were scalded in. Heat them again in the same water as before; when they are of a nice green, let them have one or two boils, take them out, and put them into cold water; drain them from this, and pour a thin syrup, made with a pound and a half of sugar to a pint of water, over them, boiling hot. Have sufficient to cover them, and let them remain in it for two or three days. Drain off the syrup into a preserving-pan; add half a pound more sugar to each pint of water that was used; boil, scum, and pour it boiling hot over the fruit. After three or four days, or a week, pour off the syrup, and boil it again, adding a little more sugar to make it of a consistence to draw into rather a strong thread between the finger and thumb, which will be when nearly three pounds of sugar have been used to the pint. Pour this over them boiling hot; cover them over when cold, and put them away for use. Keep in a cool, dry place. They may be greened by allowing them to remain covered with leaves in the water they were first scalded in for three or four days, or until it is quite sour; then taken out, drained dry, and heated in the first syrup.

Magnum bonum, mussel, and other plums, when green, should be preserved as these.

GOOSEBERRIES.

Take the rough-skinned fruit when quite dry, with rather more than their weight of sugar pounded fine; lay a layer of fruit and a layer of sugar, till all are in the pan; add a teaspoonful of water, and boil the fruit quickly until it is clear; take it out, and put it into jars; boil up the syrup until it is thick, then pour it over the fruit. When cold, cover it closely.

PEACHES, WHOLE (AN ECONOMICAL WAY).

To fifteen pounds of cling-stone peaches take seven and a half pounds of loaf sugar; put two or three quarts of water in the kettle with one teaspoonful of pearlash, to destroy the skins of the fruit. When the water is hot, throw in a few peaches, and let them remain a few minutes; take them out, and wipe off the skins with a coarse towel, and then throw them into cold water. Take half the sugar, with as little water as possible to dissolve it; then put in a layer of peaches, and let them boil from twenty to thirty minutes. Take them out on a flat dish to cool. After two or three layers have been boiled in this way the syrup will increase; by degrees add the rest of the sugar. When all are done, boil the syrup until it becomes a little thick; then add, while in the kettle, half a pint of alcohol, which will cool and thicken it sufficiently to put on the peaches, which should be ready in your jars; do not cover them until the next day. They will not have the least taste of the alcohol, and are a very fine preserve.

PEACHES.

The clear-stone yellow peaches, white at the stone, are the best. Weigh the fruit after it is pared. To each pound of fruit allow a pound of loaf sugar. Put a layer of sugar at the bottom of the preserving-kettle, and then a layer of fruit; and so on, until the fruit is all in; stand it over hot ashes until the sugar is entirely dissolved; then boil them until they are *clear;* take them out piece by piece, and spread them on a dish free from syrup. Boil the syrup in the pan until it jellies. When the peaches are cold fill the jars half full with them, and fill up with the boiling syrup. Let them stand a short time covered with a thin cloth; then put on brandy-paper, and cover them close with corks, skin, or paper. From twenty to thirty minutes will generally be sufficient to preserve them.

BRANDY PEACHES.

To six pounds of the fruit, peeled, put three pounds of loaf sugar and three pints of white French brandy. Put them in a jar tightly corked, and boil till soft in a kettle of hot water. The water should reach to the top, but not over the top of the jar.

QUINCES.

Peel the quinces, and clear the cores out well, saving all the seeds. Wash the peelings well, and put them on to boil; let them boil until the water partakes strongly of the flavor of the quinces; put the seeds in a linen bag, and boil them with the parings. Put the quinces in a separate pan, and let them boil until *almost* tender. Strain all the quince water; put one pint of the water to each pound of fruit and sugar; boil the quinces until they are quite clear; then put them on dishes cleared from the syrup. Boil the syrup till it jellies with the bag of seeds, from which the substance should be pressed in the jelly.

It is well to add two or three pints of quince water, and two or three pounds of sugar more than is required for the fruit, for floating islands, etc.

GREEN GINGER.

For two weeks put the ginger every night and morning in fresh boiling water. Take off the outside skin with a sharp knife; boil it in water till it is quite tender, and slice it thin; prepare a syrup of one pound of sugar to half a pint of water, clarify it, and then put the ginger into it. Boil it until it is clear.

APPLES, WHOLE.

Make a syrup of loaf sugar, allowing a pound of pleasant sour apples to a pound of sugar. Be very particular in skimming it until it is quite clear. The apples should be pared very nicely, and their cores extracted, with an instrument made for the purpose, before they are weighed. Boil the apples in as much water as will cover them until they become soft; but take care that they do not commence to break. Those that cook first should be removed on a strainer until they are all tender. Squeeze the juice of one large lemon for every pound of loaf sugar. Pare off the lemon-peel, if possible, without breaking it; boil the juice and the peel in the same water that has boiled the apples; pour in the syrup as soon as the lemon-peel is tender, and boil it ten minutes, or till it is a strong syrup. The apples which have been cooling on a dish should then be gently put in jars, and the hot syrup poured on them. Tie up the jars, and do not open them for a fortnight.

CRAB APPLES.

Make a syrup, allowing the same weight of sugar as apples. Let it cool, then put in the apples, a few at once, so that they will not crowd and break to pieces. Boil them till they begin to break; then take them out of the kettle. Boil the syrup in the course of three or four days, and turn it while hot on to the apples. This continue to do at intervals of two or three days, till the apples appear to be thoroughly preserved.

PEARS.

Pare them very thin, and simmer in a thin syrup; let them lie a day or two. Make the syrup richer, and simmer again, and repeat this till they are clear; then drain, and dry them in the sun or a cool oven a very little time. They may be kept in syrup, and dried as wanted, which makes them more moist and rich.

PUMPKINS.

Choose a thick yellow pumpkin which is sweet; pare, take out the seeds, and cut the thick part into any form you choose—round, square, egg-shaped, stars, wheels, &c.; weigh it; put it into a stone jar or deep dish, and place it in a pot of water to boil, till the pumpkin is so soft that you can pass a fork through it. The pot may be kept uncovered; and be sure that no water boils into the jar. Take the weight of the pumpkin in good loaf sugar, clarify it, and boil the syrup with the juice of one lemon to every pound of sugar, and the peel cut in little squares. When the pumpkin is soft, put it into the syrup, and let it simmer gently about an hour, or till the liquor is thick and rich; then let it cool, and put it in glass jars, well secured from the air. It makes a very rich sweetmeat.

LEMON.

An excellent substitute for jam may be made as follows:— One pound of powdered loaf sugar, a quarter of a pound of fresh butter, six eggs, leaving out the whites of two of them; the juice and rind of three fine lemons. Put the ingredients into a saucepan, and stir the whole gently over a slow fire until it becomes as thick as honey. Put it into small jars, and keep it in a cool, dry place.

ORANGES AND LEMONS WHOLE.

Make a syrup of three pounds of sugar-candy in one quart of water; put good and sound oranges in this, and then boil very slowly till the liquid is reduced to one-half. Lemons may be treated in the same way. When cold and put away in jars, stir in a wineglassful of rum for every pint made. N. B.—They will not " keep " long, unless under lock and key.

SIBERIAN CRABS.

Prick each apple two or three times with a fork, and throw them into a pan of water. Simmer them either in water or a very weak syrup made with a pound of sugar to a pint and a half of water. When the skins begin to crack, take them from the fire, strain the syrup or water from them, and put them into jars. Cover them with a weak syrup whilst boiling hot, made with a pound and a half of sugar, with a pint of water. In three or four days pour off the syrup, boil it again with six or eight ounces more sugar to each pint of water used, and pour over whilst boiling. Repeat this three times, and put them aside for use. Examine them in about three or four weeks, and if there is the least indication of fermentation pour off the syrup; boil it as before with more sugar; take off any scum; give the apples a boil in the syrup; fill the jars, and tie them over with paper or bladder when cold.

SUMMER FRUITS.

Such fruits as strawberries, raspberries, blackberries, and the like, may be preserved in the following manner cheaply, and their flavor be retained:—Put sugar over the fire, at the rate of half a pound to a pound of berries, add a little water, and when hot take up the fruit in a skimmer and dip it into the sugar, holding it there for half a minute perhaps; then take it out and spread it on the tins. Go through the whole lot in this manner. Then boil down the sugar to a thick syrup, and pour it over the fruit. Set the tins either in the sun or in a warm oven till the berries are dried through in thin gelatinous cakes. When thoroughly dry put the cakes in a bag and hang it out of the way. The cakes will keep as long as wanted, and may be used in a few minutes by the addition of a little hot water—more sugar being added if necessary. The beauty of this mode is that the flavor of the fruit is retained, while there is no danger of its spoiling by fermentation. Fruits, when preserved in the usual way—pound for pound—are made too sweet, and lose their distinctive flavor so much that it differs little whether it is preserved peach or potato. Besides, without care, preserves are apt to ferment and spoil.

BOTTLED FRUIT.

FOR TARTS, WITHOUT SUGAR.

Take wide-mouthed glass, or, if possible, stone bottles; fill them by shaking, or even, if you like, by pressing them with a round stick like a ruler. Then cork them tight with the best corks (for good corking is more than half the battle), using good deep chives as they are called; wire down the cork strongly, and insert a small slip of wood between the wire and cork. Place the bottles upright in a boiler filled with cold water, up to their neck; heat the water until it boils; keep it boiling ten minutes, and then withdraw the fire, or move the boiler off it. When the water is cool, take out the bottles, and they will keep for years. They may be rosined; but with good corks it is needless, and is afterwards troublesome.

CHERRIES, ETC.

Take the common red cherries, and remove the stones. Put them in wide-mouthed, light glass bottles. Then set the bottles in a boiler of cold water, within an inch or so of the neck. Let them boil from fifteen to twenty minutes. Put the corks in the bottles as tightly as possible while the water is boiling. Then take out the bottles, tighten the corks, and seal them with a wax made of equal quantities of rosin and beeswax. This method has proved quite satisfactory. The *rationale* of the process will be readily perceived. The heat coagulates the albumen of the fruit, and arrests all change which may have taken place by the absorption of oxygen, and at the same time expels the air from the bottles. The corks, being put in while the bottles are filled with steam, and quickly tightened and sealed, effectually exclude the air, and with it all exciting cause of fermentation. The reason why the bottles are placed in cold water is to prevent them from breaking. If tin cans are used there will be no need of this precaution. Sometimes, too, the bottles break after being taken out of the water, and it is advisable to wrap a cloth round them for a few minutes.

GREEN GOOSEBERRIES AND CURRANTS.

Green gooseberries and currants may be preserved in the same way, except that they do not need so much boiling. If the bottles are heated sufficiently to drive out most of the air by expansion, and carefully corked and sealed while hot, nothing more will be required. In fact, they are sometimes kept by simply putting them in tightly-sealed bottles without any boiling. In this case the gooseberries, not being ripe, absorb the oxygen from the small quantity of air in the bottles, without injury. If the bottles, after being sealed, are placed in hot water for a few minutes, this absorption of oxygen takes place much more rapidly with the formation of carbonic acid. Unless the fruit is quite green the former method is undoubtedly the best.

Green gooseberries are frequently preserved by placing them, when dry, in a stone jar or other vessel, and burying it in the soil, below the reach of frost.

DAMSONS.

For this purpose they should be gathered before they are quite ripe, on a dry day, and after the dew is dried off them. Bottle them as soon as possible after they are gathered, and let the bottles in which they are to be put be perfectly dry.

All bruised or damaged fruit should be carefully picked out as the bottles are being filled. When quite full, cork them with good sound corks, such as are made for the purpose (not bungs), rather slightly, and place them in a boiler or deep saucepan, with cold water to reach half way up the necks of the bottles. Heat the water gradually to the boiling point, and after being kept at this heat for two or three minutes, withdraw the fire and let them cool in the water. When quite cold, cork closely, and place them in a cool dry place for use. When preserved in this way they will be found equal to fresh fruit for pies, puddings, tarts, or any other purpose for which fresh fruit is required, and will keep good for two or three years. Filling the bottles with water is a bad practice, as it deprives the fruit of much of its flavor, and does not contribute anything to their preservation.

www.ingramcontent.com/pod-product-compliance
Lightning Source LLC
Chambersburg PA
CBHW022025080426
42733CB00007B/724